The Social Desirability Variable in Personality Assessment and Research

Allen L. Edwards
University of Washington

GREENWOOD PRESS, PUBLISHERS
WESTPORT, CONNECTICUT

Library of Congress Cataloging in Publication Data

Edwards, Allen Louis.
The social desirability variable in personality assessment and research.

Reprint. Originally published: New York : Holt, Rinehart, and Winston, 1957.
Bibliography: p.
Includes index.
1. Social desirability--Testing. 2. Personality assessment. 3. Psychological research. I. Title.
BF698.E32 1981 155.2'83 81-20141
ISBN 0-313-23245-8 (lib. bdg.) AACR2

Reprinted in 1982 by Greenwood Press,
A division of Congressional Information Service, Inc.
88 Post Road West, Westport, Connecticut 06881

Printed in the United States of America

10 9 8 7 6 5 4 3 2 1

Preface

THE STUDY OF that intangible and elusive something that we refer to as personality is one of the primary concerns of many branches of psychology. This is obviously true of clinical, social, and child psychology, and of that area of psychology concerned with individual differences of all kinds. To a certain extent, it is also becoming true of modern industrial psychology.

Some years ago, the training of the industrial psychologist may have been considered almost complete if he knew how to put together a battery of ability tests which he could then correlate with performance on the job. In post-war years, the expectations and demands of industry have given new emphasis to training in personality measurement and research. For example, in the first of two volumes describing the Employee Relations Research Program initiated by the Standard Oil Company of New Jersey and Affiliates, Mason (1955, p. 9) states: "In our personnel management research projects we are trying to measure some of the most complex and yet the most important aspects of human behavior: ambition, motivation, adjustment, and other human qualities on the job."

In recent years it is possible to detect a concern for personality upon the part of those psychologists working in an area that William James once described as "brass-instrument" psychology. Personality variables have most assuredly entered into the "new look" experiments in perception and learning. It is no longer unusual, for example, to find some investigators attempting to account for the results of a perceptual or learning experiment in terms of whether the subjects are anxious or nonanxious (Mandler and Sarason, 1952; Sarason, Mandler, and Craighill, 1952; Taylor and Spence, 1952), copers or avoiders (Mainord, 1956; Schlesinger, 1954), sensitizers or defenders (Blum, 1954, 1955; Lazarus, Eriksen, and Fonda, 1951; McGinnies, 1949), sharpeners or levelers (Holzman, 1954; Holzman and Klein, 1954), secure or insecure (Hastings, 1952).

As a matter of fact, interest in personality is so widespread among the behavioral sciences that it would be pretentious to regard it as the province of the psychologist alone. The sociologist, the cultural anthropologist, the economist, the political scientist, and the educationist share the interest of the psychologist in the study of personality.

As in any scientific endeavor, if something is to be studied and investigated, means must be developed for observing and measuring the thing of interest. Procedures for observing and measuring personality variables have been described in several books (Eysenck, 1952; Ferguson, 1952; Vernon, 1953) devoted primarily to this subject. None of these books, however, gives serious consideration to what I have come to call the social desirability variable in personality assessment and research.

I use the term social desirability in two interrelated ways. In the one instance, I have reference to the social desirability scale values of personality statements. Social desirability scale values of personality statements can be obtained by any of the various psychological scaling methods that have been developed (Edwards, 1957; Green, 1954; Guilford, 1954). In the second instance, I have reference to the tendency of subjects to attribute to themselves, in self-description, personality statements with socially desirable scale values and to reject those with socially undesirable scale values.

The potentially distorting influence of this tendency on scores based on subjects' responses to statements in personality inventories has long been recognized by many psychologists. Yet, as late as 1946, Meehl and Hathaway (1946) could stress that, despite good reasons for believing in the existence of the tendency, very few systematic efforts had been directed toward doing anything about it. Their own work on the problem is one of the notable exceptions.

I became seriously interested in the problem of social desirability in 1951—and quite by accident. It was my intention, stimulated by a year's association with L. L. Thurstone, to investigate the interrelationships between various measures of attitudes and personality traits. I had no desire to develop new instruments, but instead anticipated making use of those already in existence. However, upon examination of the existing personality inventories, I found any number designed to measure such traits as "neuroticism, emotional stability, inferiority feelings, emotional maturity, neurasthenia, anxiety neurosis, hysteria, paranoia, hypomania, depression," and the like, but relatively few that would provide measures of the "normal" personality variables in which I was interested and which seemed relevant to my research. It was at this point that I felt the need to develop an inventory that would provide measures of the variables of interest to me. And it was at this point also that I had to face the problem of social desirability as a factor potentially influencing responses to statements in personality inventories and to determine what could be done about it.

My first paper on the subject of social desirability was presented to the Western Psychological Association in 1952 and published a year later under the title "The Relationship between the Judged Desirability of a Trait and the Probability that the Trait Will be Endorsed" 1953*a*). Since that time a great deal of additional research upon the subject of social desirability has been completed. In the spring of 1956, I had an opportunity to bring together and to summarize briefly the results of these studies in my Presidential Address to the Western Psychological Association. This monograph is a revision and elaboration of that paper. I wish to acknowledge my indebtedness to my students and to other psychologists who, through their research, have contributed to the content of the monograph.

The problems and implications arising from the research on the social desirability variable are many. A number of conclusions are presented which appear to be well substantiated, whereas others must be recognized as tentative and speculative. I hope that what I have to say will stimulate research designed to provide additional information as to how the social desirability variable operates, not only in personality assessment but also in experimental studies in which personality variables are a prime consideration.

For permission to quote freely from an article published previously in *Educational and Psychological Measurement,* I am indebted to G. Frederick Kuder, editor of the journal, and to Paul Horst, co-author of the article.

An appointment as a Faculty Research Fellow of the Social Science Research Council (1951–54) and a grant from the Graduate Research Committee of the University of Washington (1955) provided assistance in undertaking some of the research to be reported.

William Stellwagen has assisted in many of the calculations reported, and Louise B. Heathers has kindly made available MMPI test records used in calculating various correlations. I am grateful to both of them for their assistance.

Seattle, Washington — Allen L. Edwards

Contents

List of Figures

List of Tables

THE SOCIAL DESIRABILITY VARIABLE IN PERSONALITY ASSESSMENT AND RESEARCH

I

Introduction

IT HAS BEEN said by Klineberg (1954, p. 50) that "vocabulary may mirror the interests of a people." He points, for example, to the exceptional importance of the camel in Arab civilization and states that in Arabic there are some 6,000 words relating to camel. Something similar occurs with respect to personality in the English language. Allport and Odbert (1936) list close to 18,000 words relating to ways in which people are said to differ. The responsibility for all these descriptive terms cannot be placed upon psychologists, but there is no denying that psychologists have been extremely facile and most productive in developing descriptive categories for personality.

To engage in the study of personality in any scientific way requires, of course, that we have available descriptive categories for personality. Not content with what might be called the primary descriptive categories, however, some psychologists have formulated secondary descriptions or descriptions of the descriptive categories. To borrow the words from Meehl (1954), some descriptions of personality are themselves described as atomistic, static, and objective, whereas others are described as global, dynamic, and subjective. Fortunately, for all of us, these secondary descriptions are not of significance to the subsequent discussion. Instead, we shall be concerned with the primary descriptions themselves.

What constitutes a primary description? Opinions of psychologists vary on this question, and some choice is involved. The primary unit of personality description that I have chosen to work with is a statement about a person. My reason for this choice is quite simple. I believe that a complete description of an individual's personality would consist of all statements that appropriately characterize him. Having available a complete or partially complete description of various individuals in terms of a collection of such statements, we might then attempt to group the individuals in terms of psychiatric classifications or other typologies. Even such classifications, however, result in statements about persons. To say "He is an obsessive-compulsive personality" is to make a statement about a person, even though this statement may involve a judgment based on a variety of other statements that are used to characterize the individual. I know of no more convenient unit of personality description to work with than a statement about a person, despite the fact that some such statements may themselves subsume a variety of other statements about a person.

Statements about a person may refer to physical characteristics, interests, behavior, attitudes, traits, likes, feelings, motives, abilities, defense mechanisms, or any of the other categories we ordinarily use in describing people. Statements of the kind I have in mind are perhaps exemplified by items in personality inventories. They are, however, by no means limited to the statements found in such inventories. A clinical psychologist may describe a person by saying "He exercises overrigid intellectual control of his inner impulses." The source of this statement may come from interpretation of a Rorschach protocol or from a clinical interview. We need not be concerned with the source of the statement. As long as the statement is used to describe a person, it qualifies as one of the units in which we are interested.

Nor do we need to limit the units of description to statements that may be made by one person about another person. The same units may be used for purposes of self-description or self-assessment. Not only may the clinical psychologist describe another person with the statement "He is easily embarrassed," but the person himself may use this same statement in first person form in self-description.

Consider now the population of statements that might be used in describing personality. It is my contention that each of these statements can be characterized in terms of its position on a single dimension. I call this dimension the social desirability-undesirability dimension or, more briefly, the social desirability dimenson. I believe, for example, that it is possible to obtain a scale value for any personality statement such that the scale value indicates the position of the statement on the social desirability continuum, relative, of course, to other statements. It should be emphasized that I am *not* saying that these same statements may not fall along various other dimensions. I *am* contending that regardless of the multidimensional nature of personality statements, with respect to content, it is still possible to describe each one in terms of its position on the social desirability continuum. The social desirability continuum appears to me to be the most important single dimension on which to locate personality statements. The importance of the dimension rests in the fact that, if we know the position of a statement on it, we can then predict, with a high degree of accuracy, the proportion of individuals who will say, in self-description, that the statement does describe them.

How does one go about locating personality statements on the social desirability continuum? Any of the psychological scaling methods now available can be used for this purpose. These methods are described by Edwards (1957), Guilford (1954), and Green (1954). In my own research, I have used the method of paired

TABLE I

Instructions Used in Obtaining Judgments of Social Desirability for Personality Statements

Trait Rating Schedule

Your Name: ______________________ Age: ______ Sex: ______

Below you will find an example of four things that a person says that he likes or would like to do. These likes are called traits. Underneath the list of four traits and opposite the numbers corresponding to each of the traits are nine boxes. These boxes represent different degrees of desirability or undesirability of each trait as it appears in others, as indicated by the adjective at the top. A judge, such as yourself, has made an estimate of the degree of desirability or undesirability of these traits in people by placing an X in the box opposite each trait.

Example: 1. To like to punish your enemies.
2. To like to read psychological novels.
3. To like to make excuses for your friends.
4. To like to go out with your friends.

Trait	*Undesirable*								*Desirable*
	Extreme	Strong	Moderate	Mild	Neutral	Mild	Moderate	Strong	Extreme
1.		X							
2.					X				
3.							X		
4.								X	

The person who judged these traits believes that "to like to punish your enemies" is a definitely undesirable trait in others, "to like to read psychological novels" is neither desirable nor undesirable, "to like to make excuses for your friends" is moderately desirable, and "to like to go out with your friends" is quite a desirable trait in other people.

Indicate your own judgments of the desirability or undesirability of the traits which will be given to you by the examiner in the same manner. *Remember that you are to judge the traits in terms of whether you consider them desirable or undesirable in others.* Be sure to make a judgment about each trait.

comparisons, the method of successive intervals, and the method of equal-appearing intervals to obtain social desirability scale values for personality statements.* Just as many investigators have used these methods to scale attitude statements for degree of favorableness or unfavorableness, so I have used them to scale personality statements for degree of social desirability or social undesirability. Table 1 gives the instructions we have used in several studies.

I hope that this brief discussion will make clear that, when I refer to the social desirability scale value of a personality statement, I mean its location on the continuum of social desirability as determined by one of the various psychological scaling methods. High scale values will represent statements that are judged as highly socially desirable, and low scale values will represent statements that are judged as socially undesirable, with reference, of course, to an arbitrary origin of average social desirability.

* Since I shall frequently refer to the method of equal-appearing intervals and the method of successive intervals, it is well to differentiate now between these two psychological scaling methods. The method of successive intervals is a scaling method devised by Thurstone subsequent to his development of the method of equal-appearing intervals. The latter method assumes that each of the successive intervals is equal in width. In successive-interval scaling, equality in width of successive intervals is not assumed. Both methods are described in detail by Edwards (1957) and Guilford (1954).

2

The Comparability of Social Desirability Scale Values Derived from Different Groups of Judges

THE SOCIAL desirability scale of value of a personality statement has been defined as a value that is obtained as a result of performing certain operations upon a set of observations made under specified conditions. The observations are the judgments of social desirability made by the subjects in the judging group. The operations are those of a particular psychological scaling method. The specified conditions are the instructions given to the members of the judging group. If we have used one of the psychological scaling methods to obtain social desirability scale values for a given set of personality statements, based upon the judgments of one group, then what assurance do we have that we would obtain comparable scale values for the same statements from other groups of judges under the same judging instructions?

In obtaining judgments of social desirability, it is assumed that the judging group is representative of some defined population. There is ample evidence to indicate that the scale values of statements are comparable from group to group as long as the various groups are drawn from the same population and as long as the judging instructions are the same. It is obvious, however, that what is considered socially desirable or undesirable in the way of personality traits is culturally determined. Social desirability scale values of personality statements may, therefore, vary from culture to culture or from judging group to judging group, if the various groups are representative of different populations. We might find, in other words, different scale values for the same set of statements when the statements are judged by males or females, or by different socioeconomic groups, or by different age groups. We might also find different scale values for the same statements if we change the instructions to the judging group. In research involving the social desirability scale values of personality statements, these possibilities must always be considered.

Suppose, for example, that we have derived scale values for a particular set of statements from the judgments of a group of males. In subsequent research, a relationship is found between these scale values and other behavior of interest in another group of males. Using the male scale values, would we find a similar relationship for a group of females? If the scale values are the same for the two groups, then we should expect the relationship to hold for females as well as for males. If the relationship is not observed for the females, then we might question whether the social desirability scale values are the same for the two groups. Rescaling the statements to obtain scale values based upon the judgments of females may result in our observing the relationship we originally observed for the males.

The fact that we have found social desirability scale values to be comparable for various groups indicates that the relationships to be reported upon later may be expected to hold for each of the various groups without the necessity of rescaling the statements to obtain separate sets of scale values for each group. It is to be emphasized, however, that in these studies the instructions to the various judging groups were the same for all groups.

Figure 1, for example, indicates the similarities in scale values that would be obtained for a set of 140 statements, if we treated the

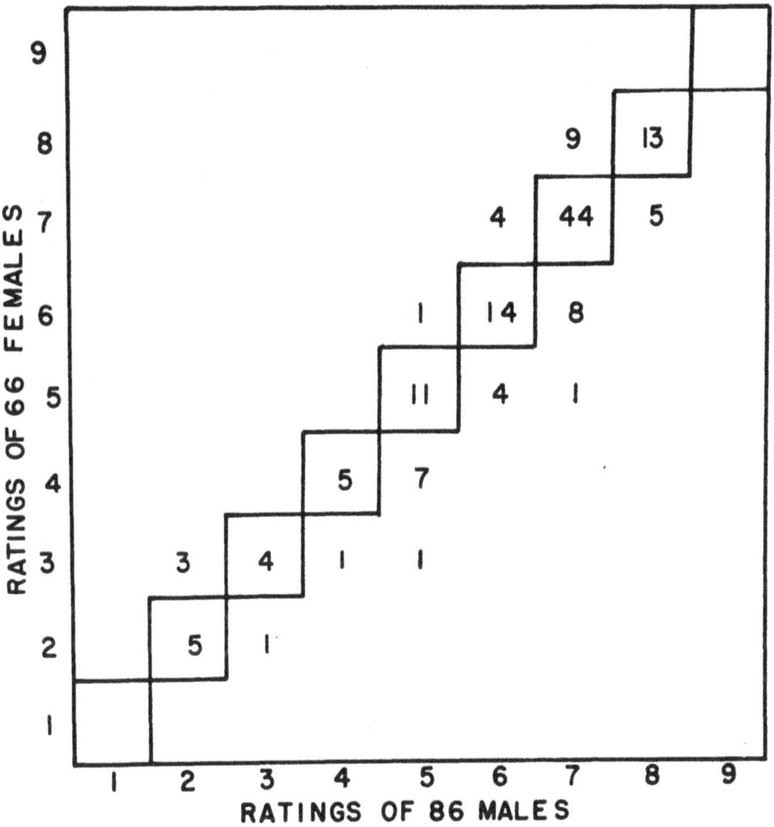

FIG. 1. *The interval in which the social desirability scale value of a statement would fall in terms of female judgments plotted against the interval in which the scale value of the same statement would fall in terms of male judgments. Statements are from the Personal Preference Schedule.* Source: *Edwards* (1953a).

judgments of males and females separately. The subjects judging the social desirability of the statements consisted of 86 men and 66 women, a total of 152 judges. Twenty-six of the judges were under 20 years of age, 97 were between 20 and 30 years of age, and 29 were over 30 years of age. All the judges were students in psychology classes, day and evening, at the University of Washington. The scale values of these statements were investigated in the initial stages of the development of a personality inventory (Edwards, 1953*a*). Figure 1 does not show the actual scale values of the statements. The actual scale values were determined by the method of successive intervals, and the figure shows only whether the scale values for a given statement, as determined by the judgments of the two groups, would fall within the same interval. We see that 95 of the 140 statements would have scale values within the same interval, regardless of whether the scale values were determined solely from the judgments of males or from the judgments of females. Only 2 of the 140 statements would have scale values separated by as much as one interval.

For many of the 43 statements falling just outside of the principal diagonal, the actual scale values may still be approximately the same, for the reason that the scale values for both groups are close to the limit of the interval, but one scale value happens to fall slightly above and the other slightly below the limit. In this respect, the manner in which the entries have been tabulated in Figure 1 exaggrates the discrepancies between the two sets of values.

Figure 2 shows that the similarity in scale values that is obtained from male and female judges is not restricted to the 140 personality statements of Figure 1. The 128 items shown in Figure 2 are from the Interpersonal Check List. The Interpersonal Check List was developed by staff members of the Kaiser Foundation Research Project in Psychology for obtaining personality assessments. It is described in an article by LaForge and Suczek (1955) and has been prepared in booklet form by Leary (1956). Ninety-one of the

128 items shown in Figure 2 would have scale values falling within the same interval, regardless of whether the scale values were determined solely from the judgments of the group of 39 college females or from those of the 55–58 college males. The number of males

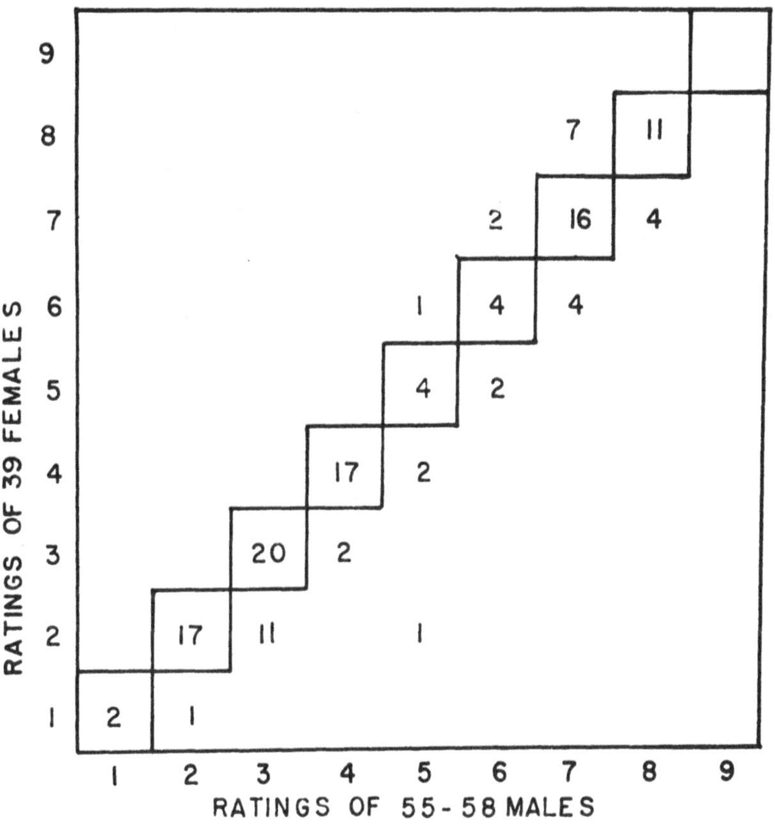

FIG. 2. *The interval in which the social desirability scale value of a statement would fall in terms of female judgments plotted against the interval in which the scale value of the same statement would fall in terms of male judgments. Statements are from the Interpersonal Check List.*

judging each item varies because of failure to obtain complete sets of judgments for all 58 judges.*

Fujita (1956) scaled personality statements from the Personal Preference Schedule for social desirability, using as judges a group of 50 Japanese-American college students. It was his belief that the culture and background of this group differed in many respects from the college group of 152 judges I originally used in scaling the same statements for social desirability. We both used the method of successive intervals in deriving scale values for the statements. In this instance we can see the similarity between these two sets of scale values somewhat better than in the previous figures, because, instead of merely showing the intervals in which the scale values fall, Figure 3 shows the plot of the scale values themselves. It is apparent that the relationship between the two sets of scale values is linear. The product-moment correlation between the two sets of values is .95.

Klett (1956) and Lovaas (1956) have also investigated the social desirability scale values of the statements in the Personal Preference Schedule. Klett's judges consisted of high-school males and females from three different socio-economic classes. He found that the standards of social desirability of high-school males and females are much the same with respect to the statements investigated. This was also true when the three socio-economic groups were compared with one another. Pooling the judgments from all his groups, Klett obtained successive interval scale values for the statements. The product-moment correlation between Klett's scale values, based upon

* When a citation is not given, the research is my own and, in general, is being reported here for the first time. The results of this particular study, however, were later prepared for journal publication (Edwards, 1958).

Kogan and Kogan (1957) have provided me with additional evidence concerning the stability of the social desirability scale values of the items in the Interpersonal Check List. They obtained judgments of social desirability for these items from a group of 15 "Skid-Row," alcoholic, TB patients and from a group of 46 neuropsychiatric patients. The scale values based upon the judgments of these two groups correlated .94 and .95 respectively with the values I originally obtained from the group of college students.

the judgments of 206 high-school students, and the values I originally obtained from judgments of 152 college students was .93.

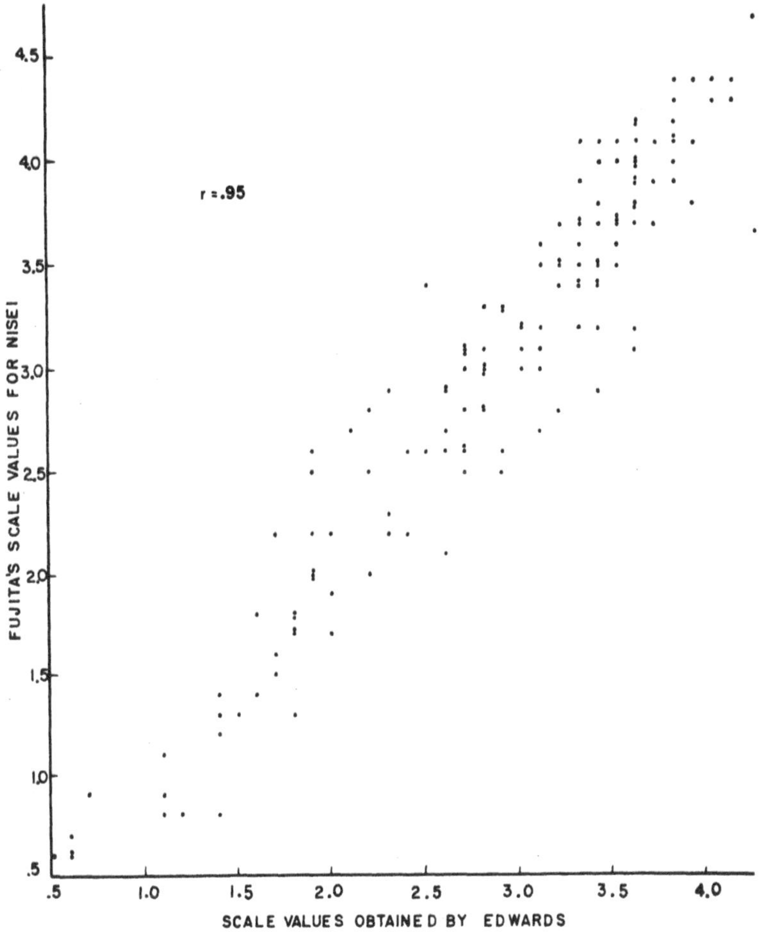

Fig. 3. *The relationship between the social desirability scale values of statements as determined by the method of successive intervals for a group of 50 Nisei and a group of 152 non-Nisei. Statements are from the Personal Preference Schedule. Source: Fujita (1956).*

Lovaas (1956) translated the statements in the Personal Preference Schedule from English into Norwegian and obtained judgments from 50 male and 36 female students at two *gymnasiums* in Oslo, Norway, in the fall of 1954. The average age of his judges was 17 years. Scale values for the statements were found by the method of successive intervals. The product-moment correlation between the scale values based upon the judgments of the Norwegian group and those based upon the American college group of 152 judges was .78.

In a study mentioned earlier (Edwards, 1953*a*), it was found that, when judges were classified into three different age groups, there was also a high degree of agreement between the groups as to the social desirability scale values of the statements in the Personal Preference Schedule. One group consisted of 26 judges under 20 years of age, the second of 97 judges between 20 and 30 years of age, and the third of 29 judges over 30 years of age.

In a study by Hanley (1956), 25 statements from the D (or Depression) scale of the Minnesota Multiphasic Personality Inventory were combined with 32 statements from the Sc (or Schizophrenia) scale of the same inventory and scaled for social desirability by a group of 87 judges. In a second experiment, with a new group of 77 judges, 29 items from the K scale of the MMPI were scaled for social desirability along with 5 non-K items from the earlier study. Six of the K items also appear in the D and Sc scales. Scale values of the 11 items common to both studies were determined separately for each of the two experiments by means of the method of equal-appearing intervals.

If we compare the two sets of scale values for the 11 items common to both experiments, we can obtain some indication of the stability of the social desirability scale values of the statements when the context in which they were judged differs. The largest single discrepancy was for MMPI Booklet Item No. 142. When scaled in the D-Sc set of items the scale value for this item was 4.0, and when scaled in the K set it was 2.6.

From data given by Hanley, the product-moment correlation between the two sets of scale values for the 11 items was calculated and found to be .99. In this instance, the context in which the 11 items were judged appears to have had little influence upon the resulting social desirability scale values.

In still another study, Klett (1957) scaled the statements in the Personal Preference Schedule for social desirability, using as judges a sample of male veterans hospitalized for neuropsychiatric disorders. The judges consisted of 118 males drawn from the admissions ward and, according to hospital records, 89 were classified as psychotic and 29 as nonpsychotic. No essential difference was observed in the judgments of the psychotic and nonpsychotic groups, and scale values for the statements were therefore based upon the judgments of the combined groups. The scale values found by means of the method of successive intervals for this group of patients correlated .88 with the scale values of the same statements based upon the judgments of 152 college students.

The studies cited would thus seem to indicate that, for the particular statements investigated, age and sex are not important variables related to the social desirability scale values of the statements. Klett's (1956) data also indicate that, as far as high-school students are concerned, socio-economic status is not an important variable related to the social desirability scale values of the statements. Nor can we, according to Klett's (1957) findings, conclude that the social desirability scale values of the statements in the Personal Preference Schedule as determined by the judgments of neuropsychiatric patients are unrelated to the scale values of the same statements based upon the judgments of college students.

In all these studies, however, the instructions to the judging group were similar to those given in Table 1. One might assume that these instructions tend to produce a set in which judgments of social desirability are made in terms of fairly general cultural norms of social desirability. Although no research has been done upon the problem of varied instructions to the judging group, it seems reasonable to assume that different scale values for the same group of statements would be obtained if the set induced by the instructions had reference to more specific norms of social desirability. For example, if the judges had been instructed to make their judgments in terms of what they considered socially desirable traits for a physician, a salesman, a professor, or for some other specific occupational group, the scale values thus obtained would not necessarily be comparable to those obtained by the more general instructions concerning social desirability. Indeed, if the personality traits considered desirable in physicians differ from those considered desirable in people in general, we would expect little correlation between the scale values obtained under the different sets of instructions.

3

Probability of Endorsement and Social Desirability Scale Value

I NOW WANT to report upon the relationship between the social desirability scale value of a personality statement and the probability that this statement will be endorsed by subjects when they are asked to describe their own personalities in terms of the statement. For example, assume that we have scaled a set of personality statements so that we have available for each one a scale value on the social desirability continuum. These statements are then printed in the form of a personality inventory. The inventory is administered to a new and independent group of subjects with the usual instructions. By new and independent group I mean one other than that used in determining the social desirability scale values of the statements. For this new group of subjects we find the proportion endorsing each statement, that is, the proportion who say that a given statement is applicable in self-description. Each of these proportions may be regarded as a probability that a given statement will be answered "Yes," or "Agree," or "True," depending upon the form of the inventory.

A set of 140 personality statements was judged for social desirability by a group of 152 judges (Edwards, 1953*a*). Scale values for the statements were obtained by the method of successive intervals. The statements were then printed in inventory form, and the inventory was administered to a new group of 140 students. One of the statements in the inventory was "I like to be loyal to my friends." This statement had an extremely high social desirability scale value (4.14) on the successive interval continuum, and it was endorsed by 98 per cent of the students. Another statement in the inventory was "I like to avoid responsibilities and obligations." This statement had an extremely low social desirability scale value (0.68) on the successive interval continuum and it was endorsed by only 6 per cent of the students.

For the complete set of statements it was found that, as the social desirability scale value of the statements increased, so also did the per cent endorsing the statements. Figure 4 shows the relationship between probability of endorsement and social desirability scale value for the 140 statements. It is evident that probability of endorsement is linearly related to social desirability scale value. The product-moment correlation between the two variables shown in Figure 4 is .87.

Calvin Wright (1957) has repeated this study with a minor variation. He gave the same 140 statements to a group of 127 college students. Approximately half of the students in the group were males and the other half females. He asked the students to rate the degree to which each statement characterized them on a 9-point scale. For each of the statements he found the mean rating assigned in self-description. These means were then correlated with the social desirability scale values of the statements. The correlation between the two variables, for this sample, was .88.

Earlier I discussed briefly the Interpersonal Check List in connection with the agreement between the judgments of males and females as to the social desirability scale values of the 128 items in the check list. By pooling the judgments of males and females social desirability scale values were obtained for the items by means of the method of equal-appearing intervals. The statements were then given

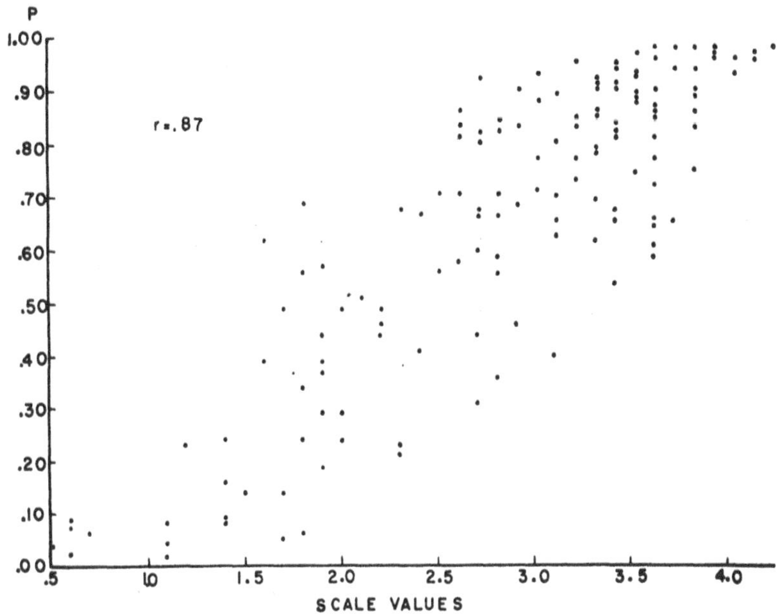

FIG. 4. *Probability of endorsement of a personality statement as related to the social desirability scale value of the statement. Statements are from the Personal Preference Schedule. Source: Edwards (1953a).*

to a new group of 67 females and 66 males for purposes of self-description. All the subjects were students in speech classes at the University of Washington.

In this instance, I wanted to determine whether the relationship between probability of endorsement of a personality statement and social desirability scale value of the statement would still be found when subjects were asked to make their self-descriptions anonymously.* The students were therefore instructed not to sign

* That the requirement of signing one's name to self-assessments may be a factor in the relationship observed between probability of endorsement and social desirability scale value is indicated by Meehl and Hathaway (1946). After reviewing research by Maller (1930), Olson (1936), and Spencer (1938), Meehl and Hathaway conclude that requiring subjects to sign their names to their self-assessments has been shown to have a definite influence on the scores obtained from self ratings.

their names to their self-assessments. In addition, they were told that their instructor would not see their test booklets. The purpose of the study, they were informed, was to investigate sex differences in self-ratings. I hoped, as a result of these instructions, to provide some assurance to them that their self-descriptions would indeed be anonymous.

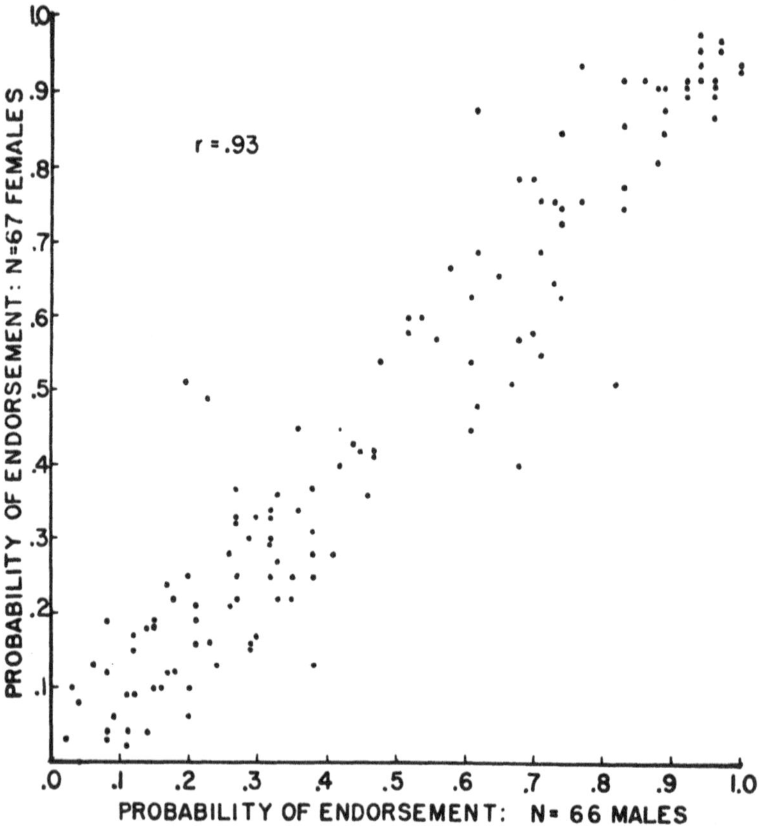

FIG. 5. *Probability of endorsement of a personality statement for a group of females as related to probability of endorsement of the same statement for a group of males. Statements are from the Interpersonal Check List.*

Figure 5 shows the probability of endorsement of an item as obtained from the female self-descriptions plotted against the corresponding probability of endorsement as obtained from the male self-descriptions. It is evident that the probability of endorsement of any given item in the check list is much the same for the two groups. The product-moment correlation between the two sets of probabilities is .93.

In Figure 6 the probability of endorsement of an item in the Interpersonal Check List for the combined group of 133 subjects is plotted against the corresponding social desirability scale value of the item. Again we find that probability of endorsement is related

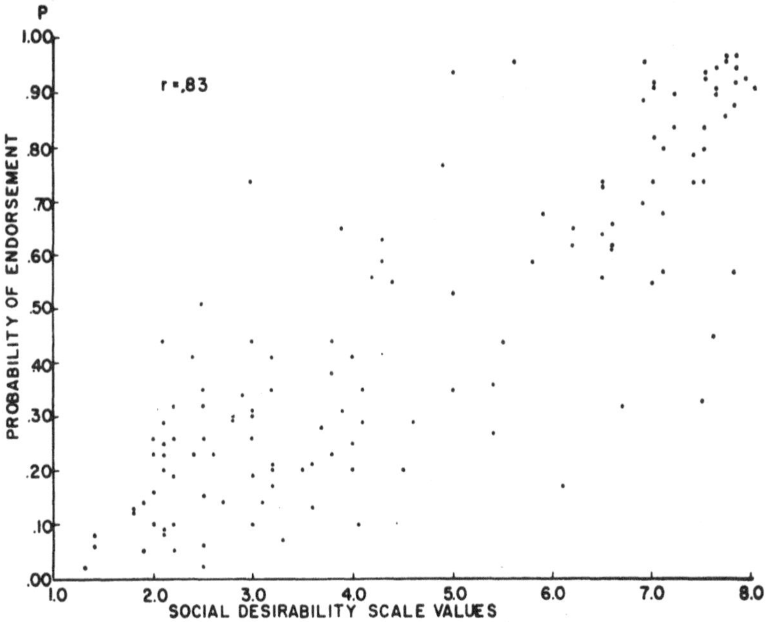

FIG. 6. *Probability of endorsement of a personality statement as related to the social desirability scale value of the statement. Statements are from the Interpersonal Check List.*

to social desirability scale value. The product-moment correlation for the data shown in Figure 6 is .83.*

The results of this study would seem to indicate that the relationship between probability of endorsement of a personality statement in self-description and social desirability scale value of the statement is not dependent upon the condition of signing one's name to one's self-assessment.

A set of 25 traits has been used by Zimmer (1954) to describe personality. Zimmer states that he selected these traits because (a) they occurred between six and ten times in one million words, as judged by the Thorndike-Lorge word count, (b) they reflected dynamic content, and (c) they do not represent "a cultural stereotype of a desirable or undesirable trait" (1954, p. 447). If Zimmer is correct with respect to his third criterion, then we might expect imperceptible differences in the social desirability scale values of these traits, with a resultant negligible relationship between social desirability scale value and probability of endorsement. We shall see that this is not the case.

Kenny (1956) has scaled Zimmer's traits for social desirability using the method of equal-appearing intervals. Judges consisted of 28 female and 39 male students at the University of British Columbia. The traits, ranked in order from most to least socially desirable, in terms of their scale values, are: respectful, energetic, orderly, refined, ambitious, trusting, spontaneous, precise, determined, obedient, economical, ardent, persistent, deliberate, cautious, conventional, leisurely, daring, sentimental, poetic, emotional, wary, dominant, meek, and lusty.

Having determined social desirability scale values for these traits, Kenny then stated them in first person form. For example, each trait was expressed in the form: "I am respectful," "I am energetic," and so on. A new and independent group of 65 college students responded to the traits in this inventory form, and for this

* The results of this study were later prepared for journal publication (Edwards, 1958).

sample the probability of endorsement was found for each trait. The rank-order correlation between probability of endorsement and social desirability scale value was .82.

In still another study, Hanley (1956) drew samples of statements from three Minnesota Multiphasic Personality Inventory (MMPI) scales. Twenty-five statements were taken at random from the 60-item D (or Depression) scale. Thirty-two other statements were drawn at random from the 78-item Sc (or Schizophrenia) scale.* These 57 statements were then judged for social desirability by a group of 44 female and 43 male students. Scale values, based upon the combined judgments of the males and females, were determined by the method of equal-appearing intervals. A new and independent sample of 106 students (64 males and 42 females) who had previously taken the MMPI served as the group for which probability of endorsement of each of the statements was obtained.

The statement with the most socially undesirable scale value was "Most of the time I wish I were dead," and this statement had a probability of endorsement of .01. A "neutral" or average statement in terms of social desirability was "I am easily awakened by noise," and the probability of endorsement for this statement was .35. The statement judged most socially desirable of all was "I loved my mother," and for this statement the probability of endorsement was .93.

The product-moment correlation between probability of endorsement for the 32 statements from the Sc scale and social desirability scale value was .89. Much the same results were obtained for the 25 statements from the D scale. In this instance, the product-moment correlation between probability of endorsement and social desirability scale value was .82.

In a subsequent study, in which probability of endorsement

* The items in the D scale were selected to measure the clinically recognized symptom complex of the depressed personality. Those in the Sc scale were selected to measure the similarity of responses of subjects to those of clinical patients classified psychiatrically as schizophrenic. More detailed descriptions of these scales are given by Hathaway and McKinley (1951).

was based upon data obtained by Hathaway from a sample of 152 college males and 113 college females, Hanley found a correlation of .92 between probability of endorsement and social desirability scale value for the 32 statements from the Sc scale. For the same sample of students, the correlation between probability of endorsement and social desirability scale value for the 25 statements from the D scale was .86.

In another study, Rosen (1956) gave subjects a shortened form of the MMPI under two conditions of administration: under the standard instructions to provide self-descriptions and under instructions to give what he has called personally desirable responses. As I shall show later, Rosen's instructions to give personally desirable responses and those I have used to obtain judgments of social desirability for personality statements are similar. The major difference between the two sets of instruction is that, whereas I have asked for a rating of the *degree* of desirability, Rosen asked for a "Yes-No" judgment of desirability.*

Taking the records of subjects obtained under the desirable instructions, Rosen counted the number answering "True" to each of the 409 items. I would assume that, the higher the social desirability scale value of an item, the more likely it is to be recognized as desirable and thus the greater the number of subjects answering "True" under Rosen's desirable instructions. These counts, therefore, may be taken as crude measures of the degree of social desirability of the items.

It has already been shown that probability of endorsement of an item under standard instructions is positively correlated with the social desirability scale value of the item. We might expect, there-

* Rosen, in other words, was interested only in determining whether a subject would consider a given statement either socially desirable or socially undesirable and not in the degree of social desirability or social undesirability of the statement. In general, I do not consider that social desirability is an all-or-none proposition, but rather that it is a matter of degree. As I have indicated earlier, even among those statements judged socially desirable, the probability of endorsement increases with the degree of social desirability. And, among those judged socially undesirable, the probability of endorsement decreases with the degree of social undesirability.

fore, that, if the counts obtained under the desirable instructions were correlated with the number answering "True" under standard instructions, a positive correlation would also be observed. Obtaining the correlations between these counts separately for males and females, Rosen, in both instances, found product-moment correlations of .87. It is a coincidence that these correlations are identical with the correlation I obtained between probability of endorsement and social desirability scale value of an item in the study (Edwards, 1953*a*) described earlier. It would have been of equal significance if the correlations had not been identical but merely comparable.

One other study may be mentioned. Navran and Stauffacher (1954) asked a group of 25 nursing students to provide self-descriptions by ranking 15 personality traits from most to least descriptive. The same group then ranked the 15 traits according to social desirability. Mean ranks were obtained for each of the traits under each of the conditions of instruction. The rank-order correlation between the mean ranks assigned to the traits in self-description and in social desirability was .90.

All the studies cited have supported the statement made earlier that probability of endorsement of an item in a personality inventory is positively and highly correlated with the social desirability scale value of the item. Some of the implications of this finding for personality assessment and research will be discussed later.

4

The SD Scale

A BRIEF DESCRIPTION of a Social Desirability (SD) scale, based upon 79 items in the MMPI, has been given elsewhere (Edwards, 1953*b*). A subsequent article by Fordyce (1956) gives the correlations between the 79-item SD scale and various clinical scales of the MMPI. Merrill and Heathers (1956) report the correlations between a short form of the SD scale, consisting of 39 items, and various scales, clinical and nonclinical, of the MMPI. Scores on the SD scale have been found to be substantially correlated with scores on a variety of personality scales. That this should be so will become readily apparent if we consider how the SD scale was developed.

A procedure frequently used in constructing attitude scales is to have a group of subjects judge the degree of favorableness or unfavorableness of the opinion expressed by each of a number of attitude statements relating to some psychological object. Upon the basis of these judgments a scale value is obtained for each statement by means of the method of equal-appearing intervals or one of the other psychological scaling methods. The scale value of a statement is taken as an indication of the location of the statement on a psychological continuum ranging from highly unfavorable, through "neutral," to highly favorable. There is adequate and ample evidence to indicate that the scale values thus obtained are highly reliable and relatively independent of the attitudes of the judges themselves toward the psychological object (Edwards, 1957).

As we have seen, a similar procedure can be applied to the kinds of statements typically contained in personality inventories. In this instance, however, we ask the group of subjects to judge the degree of social desirability or undesirability of the behavior or feeling expressed by each of the statements. The scale value of a statement, based upon these judgments, is taken as an indication of the location of the statement on a psychological continuum ranging from highly socially undesirable, through "neutral," to highly socially desirable.

There are undoubtedly individual differences in the tendency of subjects to give socially desirable responses to statements in personality inventories. The tendency itself, I believe, is manifested in the endorsement of statements with socially desirable scale values and the failure to endorse those with socially undesirable scale values. Some subjects may show this tendency to a high degree, and others may show it to a lesser degree. A score to measure the tendency could be obtained for any inventory, provided that we had knowledge of the social desirability scale values of the statements in the inventory. If a statement had a socially desirable scale value and a subject answered "Yes" to it in self-description, we would score the response 1; if a statement had a socially undesirable scale value and the subject answered "No," we would score this response 1 also. The score on the inventory would thus be the number of times the subject endorsed statements with socially desirable scale values and rejected statements with socially undesirable scale values. The responses given the weight of 1 are referred to as socially desirable responses. Any score obtained in this manner for any set of personality statements may be referred to as an SD score. The SD score is based upon the number of socially desirable responses a subject gives in self-description.

Although it is believed possible to score any existing personality inventory in the manner described, to do so would raise a number of problems. Suppose, for example, that we scored the items in an inventory designed to measure "dominance" for SD. In this instance, we would probably find the scoring key for the SD scale and that for the Dominance scale very similar. The reason for this is that dominance itself is likely to be considered a socially desirable trait. Thus the responses keyed for dominance would also be the responses keyed for SD, and scores on the SD and Dominance scales would be highly correlated. We might contend, therefore, that the SD score was a measure of dominance rather than the variable we hoped to measure, namely, the tendency of subjects to give socially desirable responses in self-description.

Furthermore, assume that subjects in responding to the statements in the inventory would not have too much difficulty in recognizing the nature of the trait supposedly measured by the inventory. If the trait is dominance, then the very wording of the statements in the inventory may enable them to make an intelligent guess as to what the inventory was designed to measure. If some of the subjects regard dominance as a socially desirable trait and others do not, their scores may reflect not only the SD variable but also their judgments of the social desirability of the trait itself.

It would seem that the items to be included in an SD scale should be quite heterogeneous in content. With a heterogeneous set of items, we might hope that each one would have to be responded to primarily on the basis of social desirability alone rather than in terms of the social desirability of some personality trait that each item in the set is supposedly measuring.

An initial set of statements was obtained from those included in a number of MMPI scales. These scales were the Anxiety Scale, the F scale, the L scale, and the K scale. Previous research by Meehl and Hathaway (1946) indicated that the three "validity" scales, F, K, and L, might be suitable for my purpose. Anxiety was believed to be a trait sufficiently vague to provide another useful pool of items.

Responses to statements in the Anxiety scale, for example, are often obtained with an inventory entitled the Biographical Inventory (Taylor, 1953).

The 150 items in these scales were submitted to a group of 10 judges who were asked to respond to each one in a socially desirable fashion, that is, to give socially desirable responses. I was not interested in obtaining exact social desirability scale values for these statements, but only in being able to select a set for which there was clear-cut agreement as to what the socially desirable response should be. For 79 of the 150 statements I found perfect agreement that a particular response, either "Yes" or "No," was the judged socially desirable response. The probability that such agreement would occur by chance, if it is assumed that a "Yes" or "No" response is equally likely, is, of course, less than .001 for a single item. This would seem to indicate that there was little doubt among the judges as to the socially desirable response for these 79 items, and little need for obtaining judgments from a larger group. The 79 items are fairly varied in content, but there is nothing subtle about them when we assume the social desirability frame of reference.

The 79 items thus obtained became the first SD scale. The scoring key was based upon the judgments of the original group of 10 judges. For a sample of 106 college students, I found the mean score on the 79-item SD scale to be 67.0 with a standard deviation of 8.2. This is the scale that I used in reporting the correlations between SD and the PPS variables (Edwards, 1953*b*) and that Fordyce (1956) used in reporting his correlations between SD and various clinical scales of the MMPI.

The items in the original SD scale were later analyzed and a set of 39 items selected that showed the greatest differentiation between a high and a low group in terms of total SD scores on the 79-item scale. The distribution of scores on this short form of the SD scale is somewhat negatively skewed. For a sample of 84 male students, I found a mean of 28.6 and a standard deviation of 6.5 on the 39-item SD scale and, for a sample of 108 female students, a mean of 27.1 and a standard deviation of 6.5. The medians of the two groups were 29.5 and 27.9 respectively. For the combined group of 192 students the corrected split-half reliability was .83. Since it is the 39-item SD scale that has been used in our later research, the MMPI Booklet Numbers of the statements and the scoring key are given in Table 2, along with the item overlap with various other MMPI scales.

I pointed out earlier that, if an inventory was designed to measure a personality trait that was itself considered socially desirable, then we would expect to find the SD key for the items in the inventory to be very similar to the trait key. If the inventory were scored by each key, the correlation between the two sets of scores should be quite high and positive. This should, in general, be true for all inventories designed to measure traits which are themselves considered socially desirable. Similarly, if a high score on a given personality inventory indicates a trait that would itself be judged as socially undesirable, we would expect the scoring key for SD and that for the trait to be reversed, thus producing a high negative correlation between the SD and trait scores. In both cases the observed correlations would be artifacts of the scoring keys applied to the same items; they are not independent.

By having available a separate SD scale based upon a different set of items and by correlating scores on this SD scale with those of a given personality inventory, we are no longer correlating two sets of scores which are necessarily dependent by virtue of scoring the same set of items with two keys which are not themselves independent. The meaning of any obtained correlations between scores on the SD scale and those on other personality inventories will thus have to be sought elsewhere.

If the SD scale does provide a measure of the tendency of subjects to give socially desirable responses to statements in self-description, then the correlations of scores on this scale with other personality scales, given under standard instructions, should indicate something of the extent to which the social desirability variable is operat-

TABLE 2

MMPI BOOKLET NUMBERS AND SCORING KEY FOR THE 39-ITEM SD SCALE

No.	*Key*	*No.*	*Key*	*No.*	*Key*	*No.*	*Key*	*No.*	*Key*
7	T	138	F	218	F	269	F	383	F
18	T	148	F	241	F	286	F	424	F
32	F	156	F	245	F	301	F	431	F
40	F	158	F	247	F	321	F	439	F
42	F	163	T	252	F	335	F	528	T
43	F	169	T	257	T	337	F	549	F
54	T	171	F	263	F	352	F	555	F
107	T	186	F	267	F	371	T		

ITEM OVERLAP BETWEEN THE SD SCALE AND OTHER MMPI SCALES

MMPI Scale	*No. Items in MMPI Scale*	*No. Scored Same in SD*	*No. Scored Opposite in SD*
L	15	0	0
K	30	5	0
F	64	0	12
Hs	33	0	3
D	60	2	5
Hy	60	1	5
Pd	50	2	4
Mf	60	0	0
Pa	40	0	2
Pt	48	0	5
Sc	78	0	6
Ma	46	3	2
Depend	56	0	9
Dom	28	3	0
Host	50	0	3
Si	70	0	9
Pv	50	0	4
Resp	32	0	0
Status	34	3	0
Anxiety	50	0	22

ing at the time. Table 3 gives the correlations between the SD scale and various other inventories of the self-report type. Those correlations above the line in the middle of the table are based upon the 39-item SD scale and those below upon the 79-item scale.

TABLE 3

CORRELATIONS BETWEEN THE SD SCALE AND VARIOUS PERSONALITY SCALES

MMPI Scales[1]	*39-Item SD Scale*
Gough's Dominance scale	.49
Gough's Responsibility scale	.52
Gough's Status scale	.61
Drake's Social Introversion scale	—.90
Taylor's Manifest Anxiety scale	—.84
Winne's Neuroticism scale	—.50
Cook's P-v scale	—.80
Cook's Hostility scale	—.75
Navran's Dependency scale	—.73
Maslow's S-I Inventory[2]	—.85
Guilford-Martin Scales[3]	*79-Item SD Scale*
Cooperativeness	.63
Agreeableness	.53
Objectivity	.71
Taylor's Manifest Anxiety scale[3]	—.60

[1] Merrill and Heathers (1956): $N = 155$ counseling center males: r_t.
[2] Edwards: $N = 30$ college males and females: r.
[3] Edwards (1953*b*): $N = 106$ college males and females: r.

The various scales listed in Table 3 have been named in terms of what a high score is believed to indicate. When the high score corresponds to a socially desirable characteristic, the correlation between scores on the scale and the SD scale is positive. For example, Gough's Status scale (1948), the Gough, McClosky, and Meehl scales of Dominance (1951), and Responsibility (1952), and the Guilford-Martin scales of Cooperativeness, Agreeableness, and Objectivity (undated) all have substantial positive correlations with the SD scale. When the higher score indicates what might be judged a socially undesirable characteristic, the correlation between scores on the scale and the SD scale is negative. We see this in the case of Drake's Social Introversion scale (1946), Taylor's Manifest Anxiety scale (1953), Winne's Neuroticism scale (1951), the Cook and Medley Hostility scale (1954), Navran's Dependency scale (1954), and Maslow's Insecurity scale (1952).

In a discussion of the notion of "construct validity" in psychological tests, Cronbach and Meehl (1955) have pointed out that, if two tests are presumed to measure the same construct, a correlation between them can be predicted. Knowing the manner in which the SD scale was developed, we should not have had any great difficulty in predicting the signs of the correlations shown in Table 3. It is my contention that each of the personality scales listed there is measuring, to some extent, the tendency of subjects to give socially desirable responses in self-description. Therefore, if a high score on the personality scale indicates a socially desirable trait, we should expect a positive correlation between scores on the scale and the SD scale. On the other hand, if a high score on the personality scale indicates a socially undesirable trait, we should expect a negative correlation between scores on the scale and the SD scale.

It is obvious that the scales listed in Table 3 have a substantial part of their variance in common with that of the SD scale. For example, the absolute magnitude of seven of the correlations exceeds .71. For these seven scales the correlations with the SD scale approach in magnitude the values we might expect to find for the reliability coefficients of the scales.

The manner in which the SD scale was constructed seems to indicate that it is primarily a measure of the tendency to give socially desirable responses in self-description. It would appear that this tendency is operating with respect to all the inventories listed in Table 3 and, for many of them, to a considerable degree.

However, one may question the interpretation I have given the

SD score. An examination of the scoring key for the 39-item SD scale, for example, indicates the possibility of an alternative interpretation of scores on the SD scale. It will be noted that, of the 39 items, 30 or approximately 77 per cent are keyed "False." It has long been recognized by those who have constructed personality and attitude scales that approximately half of the statements in the scale should be keyed in one direction and the other half in the opposite direction. In this way, one hopes to avoid the confounding of scores with a particular kind of response set, namely, the tendency to respond consistently in terms of "True" or "False" regardless of the content of the items themselves.

If a majority of the items in an inventory are keyed "True," for example, a high score may be measuring not only the variable we hope to measure, but also the tendency of the subject to acquiesce, that is, to respond "True." Similarly, if a majority of the items in the scale are keyed "False," then high scores may not only be measuring the variable of interest but also the tendency of the subject to dissent, that is, to respond "False."

As a matter of convenience, I shall, following Cronbach's (1946, 1950) use of the term, refer to both of these tendencies, that is, to acquiesce (respond "True") or to dissent (respond "False"), as response sets. To distinguish these response sets from the tendency of subjects to give socially desirable responses in self-description (regardless of whether the socially desirable response is "True" *or* "False"), I shall refer to the latter tendency as the SD set.

Since 30 of the 39 items in the SD scale are keyed "False," it might be argued that the SD scale is measuring the tendency of subjects to dissent with personality statements in self-description. If we assumed that the SD scale is measuring this response set, what sort of predictions would we make with respect to the correlations between scores on the SD scale and those on other personality inventories? For those personality inventories in which a substantial majority of the items are keyed "True," we would predict that the correlations will be negative. For those scales in which a substantial majority of the items are keyed "False," we would predict that the correlations will be positive. How well would we do in our predictions of the correlations between the SD scale and the various scales of the MMPI on the basis of the response set hypothesis?

We would do quite well on those scales of the MMPI in which a substantial majority of the items are keyed "True" *and* where a high score would be regarded as socially *undesirable*, as, for example, in the case of the Sc scale where 78 per cent of the items are keyed "True." We would also do quite well on those scales in which a substantial majority of the items are keyed "False" *and* where a high score would be regarded as socially *desirable* as, for example, in the case of the Dominance scale where 75 per cent of the items are keyed "False."

So far the response set hypothesis is respectable. But consider those scales in which a majority of the items are keyed "False" *and* a high score would be regarded as socially *undesirable*. There are three scales, Hs, D, and Hy, all of which have 67 per cent or more of their items keyed "False" and on which high scores would be regarded as socially undesirable. According to the response set hypothesis, we should predict positive correlations between these scales and the SD scale. The response set predictions, of course, would be in error. The SD hypothesis, on the other hand, would correctly predict that the correlations will be negative.

The response set hypothesis fails us also on those scales in which the keyed responses are fairly equally divided between "True" and "False," since in these cases, it leads to no prediction. There are four such scales, Pd, Mf, Status, and Si, with 52, 53, 56, and 50 per cent of the items keyed "False" respectively. It is difficult to see how the response set hypothesis could be used to predict the correlations betwen these scales and SD. The SD hypothesis, on the other hand, does enable us to predict the direction of the correlations, and the predictions are, in fact, borne out by the data.

Additional evidence against the response set hypothesis is provided by results obtained with two other SD scales I have worked with. One of these, which I shall refer to as a Balanced SD (BSD) scale, consists of 44 MMPI items of which 22 are keyed "True" and 22 are keyed "False." On the basis of a response set hypothesis no predictions at all can be made with respect to the nature of correlations to be expected between scores on the BSD scale and on other personality scales. This is not the case, however, for the SD hypothesis. The SD hypothesis results in the same predictions for the BSD scale as for the original 39-item SD scale. And, again, the predictions would be correct.

I shall not present all the evidence, but only the correlations relating to two MMPI scales, Sc and D. The Sc scale, it will be recalled, has 78 per cent of its items keyed "True," whereas the D scale has 67 per cent of its items keyed "False." The product-moment correlation between scores on the BSD scale and the Sc scale for a sample of 155 counseling center males is —.86. For the same sample, the correlation between the original SD scale and the Sc scale is —.80. The correlation between the two SD scales is .85, a value that is approximately the same as the corrected split-half reliability (.83) of the original SD scale as found with another sample of 192 college students. The correlation between the D scale and the BSD scale is —.52 for the sample of 155 males. The original SD scale correlates, for the same sample, —.61 with the D scale.

The second experimental SD scale I have referred to above consists of 39 items all of which are keyed "True" for social desirability. Let us call this the True SD (TSD) scale. If it can be claimed that the original SD scale (in which 30 of the 39 items are keyed "False") is a measure of the response set to dissent or respond "False," the TSD scale can also be claimed to measure the response set to acquiesce or respond "True." We should, therefore, expect the two scales to correlate negatively in terms of a response set hypothesis. They, of course, do not. The correlation between the two scales, for the sample of 155 subjects, is .70. For the same sample the TSD scale correlates —.64 with the Sc scale and —.57 with the D scale.

The evidence presented above seems to indicate that we cannot account for the correlations between the SD scale and other personality scales on the basis that the SD scale is measuring a response set of dissent. To attempt to do so results in various predictions that are not in accord with those based upon the SD hypothesis. And for these cases we have found that the predictions based upon the SD hypothesis are correct, whereas those based upon the response set hypothesis are incorrect.

Furthermore, the response set hypothesis leads to no predictions in the case of personality scales having an equal number of "True" and "False" keyed items. We can, however, predict on the basis of the SD hypothesis for these cases, and quite accurately. When we consider the BSD scale, we again have no basis for predicting the correlations between scores on this scale and various other scales in terms of the response set hypothesis. The SD hypothesis, on the other hand, does enable us to predict the correlations to be expected between the BSD scale and other personality scales. Finally, consider the fact that the response set hypothesis would result in a prediction of a positive correlation between the TSD scale and the Sc scale, whereas this correlation, as predicted by the SD hypothesis, is negative.

If we cannot account for SD in terms of a response set, can we account for the response set in terms of SD? I believe we can, at least in the case of personality inventories. Consider again a scale such as the Sc scale where a substantial majority of the items are keyed "True" and where a high score would be regarded as socially undesirable. Can we say then that the Sc scale is measuring the response set of acquiescence or the tendency to respond "True," irrespective of item content, simply because a large number of the items are keyed "True"? The fact that the TSD scale, in which all items are keyed "True," correlates negatively with scores on the Sc scale appears to offer evidence to the contrary.

Response set does not seem to be so much a matter of whether a personality scale has a large number of items keyed in the same direction, but rather a matter of the relationship between the keyed responses and the social desirability scale values of the items. I have previously defined a socially desirable response as the endorsement of an item with a socially desirable scale value or the rejection of one with a socially undesirable scale value. If the socially desirable responses in two inventories are, in general, keyed in opposite directions, the correlation between scores on the two inventories should be negative.

I believe that there is sufficient evidence to indicate that the tendency to give socially desirable responses in self-description is a fairly stable personality characteristic. Thus a subject who shows this tendency to a high degree on one personality inventory will also show it to a marked degree in his responses to items in other personality inventories. Similarly, a subject who shows the tendency to a lesser degree on one inventory will also show it to a lesser degree on other inventories. Therefore, if the socially desirable responses in two inventories are keyed in the same direction, a positive correlation should result. If the socially desirable responses in the two inventories are keyed in opposite directions, a negative correlation should result.

The items in the SD scale are all keyed for socially desirable responses. Whether the SD scale will correlate positively or negatively with scores on another inventory depends upon whether the items in the other inventory are keyed for socially desirable or socially undesirable responses and not upon whether a majority of the keyed responses are either "True" or "False." That is why, I believe, a negative correlation was found between the TSD scale and the Sc scale, despite the fact that all the items in the TSD scale are keyed "True" and a substantial majority of those in the Sc scale are also keyed "True." The responses keyed in the Sc scale are, I believe, primarily those that are socially undesirable; hence the negative correlation. A response set hypothesis could only have resulted in the prediction of a positive correlation, a prediction which is quite contrary to the fact.

5

Scale Values of Items in the Sc, D, K, and Subtle-Obvious Scales of the MMPI

As a result of a factor analysis of various MMPI scales, Wheeler, Little, and Lehner (1951) obtained a factor which has been described as a psychotic factor. According to these authors, if the psychotic factor is present to any marked degree in an individual, then he should tend to describe himself in the worst possible light. As Fordyce (1956) points out, this description of the psychotic factor closely resembles a definition of social *un*desirability. One might thus expect the loadings of the clinical scales on the psychotic factor to be comparable to the correlations of the same clinical scales with the SD scale.

TABLE 4

CORRELATIONS OF THE MMPI SCALES WITH THE SD SCALE AND THE PSYCHOTIC FACTOR

MMPI Scale	*SD Scale*[1]	*Psychotic Factor*[2]
F	—.82	—.67
K	.69	.70
Hs	—.70	—.53
D	—.69	—.48
Pd	—.57	—.70
Mf	—.21	—.38
Pa	—.60	—.63
Pt	—.86	—.94
Sc	—.91	—.92
Ma	—.50	—.62

[1] Fordyce (1956): $N = 97$ VA Np males.
[2] Wheeler, Little, Lehner (1951): $N = 110$ VA Np males. Factor signs reversed.

Table 4 shows the correlations of the SD scale with each of the MMPI scales, as obtained by Fordyce, and also the factor loadings of these scales on the psychotic factor. The factor signs have been reversed in order to make the description of the psychotic factor comparable to that of social desirability rather than social *un*desirability. One need only glance at Table 4 to observe the very close similarity between the correlations of the SD scale with the MMPI scales and the factor loadings of these same scales on the psychotic factor. The saturation of the various clinical scales with what Wheeler terms a psychotic factor but which, as Fordyce (1956, p. 174) states, "would seem to be as well labeled as social *un*desirability," suggests, according to Fordyce, "that mental illness, in a generalized sense of the term, may be characterized as involving behavior which is socially disapproved."

If the clinical scales of the MMPI do, in fact, differentiate between various diagnostic groups and a normative group, is it possible that they do so because of differences in these groups with respect to the accepted norms of social desirability? Would we find, for example, that the items in the Sc scale have different social desirability scale values for a group of schizophrenics than for a normal group? Would the Sc items, in general, have higher social desirability scale values for the schizophrenic group? If the scale values for the items in the Sc scale do differ for the two groups, would we find a linear relationship between probability of endorsement and social desirability scale value for the schizophrenic group, when their probabilities of endorsement are related to their *own* social desirability scale values? Would we find a lower or perhaps nonlinear relationship when the probabilities of endorsement for the schizophrenic group are related to the social desirability scale values of the normal group? If the items in the Sc scale do have higher social desirability scale values for schizophrenics than for normal persons and if probability of endorsement for this group is related to their own scale values of the items, would this not tend to result in a higher mean score on the scale for schizophrenics than for normal persons?

There are, I believe, a number of interesting research problems here, the results of which may add considerably to our understanding of the nature of group differences on the MMPI and other personality scales.*

Table 5 gives the correlations between the SD scale and various clinical and validity scales of the MMPI as obtained by Merrill and Heathers (1956) and by Fordyce (1956) For comparative purposes, the correlations of the K scale with the other MMPI scales, as obtained by Fordyce, are also included. Fordyce's sample consisted of 97 Np patients at a VA hospital and the group tested by Merrill and Heathers consisted of 155 counseling center clients.

The signs and magnitudes of the correlations obtained by these investigators are fairly consistent. We may also observe that, in general, the correlations between the SD scale and the clinical scales of the MMPI, shown in the first column, are slightly higher than

* See, for example, the study by Klett (1957).

TABLE 5

CORRELATIONS BETWEEN THE SD SCALE AND MMPI SCALES

MMPI Scale	*SD Scale*		*K Scale*[1]
	79 Items[1]	39 Items[2]	
L	.24	.14	.30
F	—.82	—.63	—.55
K	.69	.81	——
F-K	——	.90	——
Hs	—.70	—.52	—.60
D	—.69	—.61	—.45
Hy	—.38	.08	—.13
Pd	—.57	—.50	—.41
Mf	—.21	—.36	—.23
Pa	—.60	—.09	—.32
Pt	—.86	—.85	—.75
Sc	—.91	—.77	—.70
Ma	—.50	—.13	—.50

[1] Fordyce (1956): $N = 97$ VA Np males: r.
[2] Merrill and Heathers (1956): $N = 155$ counseling center males: r_t.

those between the K scale and the clinical scales, shown in the third column, for the same sample.

Anyone familiar with the MMPI knows that the K scale was developed in an attempt to control for a test-taking attitude. It is so described by Meehl and Hathaway (1946). The test-taking attitude of subjects may mean many different things, but it is probably safe to generalize that one of the components of this attitude is the tendency of subjects to endorse socially desirable statements and to reject socially undesirable statements. We should expect, therefore, to find scores on the K scale correlated with those on the SD scale. Table 5 indicates that this is the case. The correlation of .69 between these two variables, shown in the first column of the table, is a product-moment correlation and is based upon the 79-item SD scale. The correlation of .81, in the second column, is a tetrachoric correlation based upon the 39-item SD scale.

It should be clear, from the description of the manner in which the SD scale was constructed, that all the items in this scale have either obviously socially desirable or socially undesirable scale values. Is this true also of the Sc, D, and K scales? We may recall that Hanley (1956) scaled 32 statements from the 78-item Sc scale, 25 statements from the 60-item D scale, and 29 statements from the 30-item K scale for social desirability in terms of the method of equal-appearing intervals. Table 6 shows the distributions of these statements on the social desirability continuum.

TABLE 6

DISTRIBUTIONS OF SAMPLES OF STATEMENTS FROM THREE MMPI SCALES ON THE SOCIAL DESIRABILITY CONTINUUM[1]

Social Desirability Category	*Sc Scale*		*D Scale*		*K Scale*	
	f	P	*f*	P	*f*	P
Desirable	4	12.5	5	20.0	5	17.2
Neutral	4	12.5	7	28.0	8	27.6
Undesirable	24	75.0	13	52.0	16	55.2
TOTAL	32	100.0	25	100.0	29	100.0

[1] Hanley (1956).

Note first that the social desirability scale values of 24 or 75 per cent of the 32 Sc statements are located in the socially undesirable category. For the 25 D statements, 13 or 52 per cent have scale values in the socially undesirable category. We might conclude, therefore, that, if Hanley's sampling of the statements in these two scales is random, as he states it is, then the Sc scale is, in general, more heavily weighted with socially undesirable statements than is the D scale. Perhaps, as Hanley points out, this is one reason why the MMPI Manual reports a K correction for the Sc scale but not for the D scale.

We may recall also from the data presented in Table 5 that the correlation between the 39-item SD scale and the Sc scale is —.77, whereas the correlation of the same SD scale with the D scale is somewhat lower, —.61. This is true also for the 79-item SD scale. The difference in the magnitude of these correlations is consistent with Hanley's finding that the Sc scale contains a somewhat larger proportion of socially undesirable items than does the D scale, if it is assumed also that the keyed responses in both scales are primarily those that are socially undesirable. Is this assumption tenable?

Hanley classified the items in these two scales in terms of whether the "True" response was keyed or not keyed in determining scores on the scales. Using the dichotomy, keyed and not keyed, point-biserial correlations were obtained with social desirability scale values of the items as the continuous variable. For the D items, the point-biserial coefficient was .58 and for the Sc items it was .84. This finding also seems to indicate that the keying of the items in the D scale is somewhat less related to social desirability than it is in the Sc scale. As Hanley points out, if any tendency to answer the items in a socially desirable manner exists, the tendency will result in lowered scores on both the Sc and D scales. The reason for this is that keyed or scored responses on both scales do tend to be those that are socially undesirable.

We may observe also from Table 6 that the D scale has almost twice as many "neutral" items as the Sc scale. In this connection, it has been noted by Wiener (1948) that the Sc scale of the MMPI lacks what he has described as "subtle" items, whereas the D scale does not. It is possible, as Hanley suggests, that a subtle item in the MMPI or other personality inventories might be operationally defined as one with a scale value toward the central section of the social desirability continuum, that is, a statement that is neither obviously socially desirable nor socially undesirable.

I would extend this notion of Hanley's. In the clinical scales of the MMPI, a high score would generally be considered as indicating a high degree of a trait or variable that is itself regarded as socially undesirable. To obtain high scores on these scales, a subject must, in general, attribute to himself characteristics that would be regarded as socially undesirable, that is, give socially undesirable responses. If subtle statements are present in the clinical scales, these statements may be of such a nature that a socially desirable response is itself scored as an indication of a socially undesirable variable. Thus a subtle item in the D scale may also be one which is not necessarily "neutral" in scale value, but to which a response considered socially desirable is scored as an indication of depression.

The items in five of the MMPI scales have been classified in terms of the subtle-obvious distinction. These five scales are the D, Hy, Pd, Pa, and Ma scales. We know that total scores on these scales, the subtle-obvious distinction being ignored, are negatively correlated with scores on the SD scale. The correlations of scores on the SD scale with the separate subtle and obvious scales are not known, but evidence bearing upon the nature of the subtle-obvious distinction, as I have interpreted it, is available from a study by Rosen (1956).*

Rosen gave a shortened form of the MMPI to the same group of subjects under different instructions. In the first administration, he asked the subjects to describe themselves under the standard instruc-

* After this section was written, the correlations were calculated and made available to me by Fordyce and Rozynko (1957), clinical psychologists at the VA hospital, Seattle, Washington. They pulled a set of 50 MMPI records, obtained from male neuropsychiatric patients, from their files and calculated the product-moment correlation coefficients between scores on the 39-item SD scale and total scores on the D, Pd, Pa, Ma, and Hy scales. They then scored the subtle and obvious items in these scales separately and calculated the correlations between the SD scale and scores on the subtle and obvious scales. The correlations obtained were as follows:

MMPI Scale	*Total*	*Subtle*	*Obvious*
D	—.69	.33	—.78
Pd	—.67	.27	—.85
Pa	—.52	.06	—.72
Ma	—.08	.40	—.53
Hy	—.28	.54	—.71

In every case we find that SD correlates *negatively* and substantially with the obvious scale and *positively* with the subtle scale. The evidence thus seems to support my contention that the subtle scales contain items for which a socially desirable response is keyed. The fact that the positive correlations between SD and the subtle

tions. He also asked them to respond to the items in terms of what they believed to be personally desirable characteristics.* The exact instructions to the subjects were: "Answer 'true' if you personally think the behavior or characteristic described in each item is more desirable than undesirable in a person of your age and sex; answer 'false' if you personally think it is more undesirable than desirable" (1956, p. 152). In essence, the task set for the subjects by these instructions is that of making a judgment of what I have called the social desirability of a personality statement.

Note particularly the instructions, given in Table 1, that I have used in obtaining judgments of social desirability. My instructions also stress that judges are to make their judgments in terms of whether they consider the traits desirable or undesirable in others. The major difference between Rosen's instructions for personal desirability and those I have used to obtain judgments of social desirability is that he asks for a "Yes-No" judgment, whereas I ask for a rating of the degree of desirability or undesirability. On the basis of the judgments I obtain, and by means of one of the psychological scaling methods, I am able to derive a scale value for each personality statement. If a subject endorses (answers "True") a statement in self-description that has a socially desirable scale value, I define this as a socially desirable response, as I do also if he rejects or fails to endorse (answers "False") a statement with a socially undesirable scale value.

scales are not of the same magnitude as the negative correlations between SD and the obvious scales seems to indicate that the subtle scales contain fewer keyed socially desirable responses than the obvious scales contain keyed socially undesirable responses. Observe also the increase in the magnitude of the negative correlations between SD and the obvious scales over those based upon total scores to which the subtle items contribute.

* Slightly less than half of the subjects completed the forms on the same day, whereas the interval for the others was between one day and three weeks. According to Rosen, an analysis of variance showed no scales for which the time interval was a significant variable influencing scores on the scales obtained under conditions to give desirable responses.

Now, if the obvious scales of the MMPI contain primarily items to which a socially undesirable response is scored and if the subtle scales contain items to which a socially desirable response is scored as an indication of the variable measured by the scales, what might we expect with respect to the difference in mean scores on the subtle-obvious scales as obtained under Rosen's two conditions of administration? We would predict, I believe, that, under the instructions to give desirable responses, mean scores on the obvious scales should be lower, whereas mean scores on the subtle scales should be higher than those obtained under standard instructions. Let us examine Rosen's results to determine how successful these predictions are.

Rosen presents his data separately for males and females, and there are thus ten differences to consider on the obvious scales, five for the males and five for the females. We find that all ten of the means on the obvious scales are significantly lower under instructions to give desirable responses than under standard instructions for self-description. For the subtle scales, seven of the ten means are significantly higher under instructions to give desirable responses than under standard instructions for self-description.

It is possible that one reason why the predicted direction of the differences is not as good for the subtle scales as for the obvious scales is that, in line with Hanley's suggestion, the subtle scales contain more neutral items than do the obvious scales. We would expect responses to neutral items to be less influenced by considerations of social desirability than items which are obviously socially desirable or socially undesirable.

The above analysis suggests the possibility of controlling for the social desirability variable by developing inventories containing primarily subtle or neutral items. It may be difficult, of course, to obtain sufficient subtle or neutral items that relate to some personality variable of interest, but this is a matter for empirical investigation. Under any circumstances, it would seem to follow that, as the number of subtle or neutral items contained in a scale is increased, the relationship between probability of endorsement and social desirability scale value would decrease.

Some evidence on this point is available from Hanley's data. Table 6, for example, indicates that both the D and K scales have proportionately more statements with scale values in the neutral category than does the Sc scale. We should expect, therefore, somewhat lower correlations between probability of endorsement of the K and D items and their social desirability scale values than that observed for the Sc items. We have already found this to be true for the D items. For the K items, Hanley reports that the correlation between probability of endorsement and social desirability scale value is .50 for his original sample, and .59 for the sample of 152 college males and 113 college females provided later by Hathaway.

The K scale has long been used to correct scores on the various clinical scales of the MMPI for a test-taking attitude. If one regards the test-taking attitude as consisting primarily of the tendency to answer "Yes" to socially desirable statements and "No" to socially undesirable statements, then the SD scale may prove to be a more appropriate scale for correcting for this tendency than the K scale. I have already pointed out that all the items in the SD scale are either obviously socially desirable or socially undesirable and that the scoring key is consistent with this classification. This is not the case, however, with the K scale. All 29 of the K items investigated by Hanley are scored, in terms of the K key, only if answered "No" by the subject. Yet, Table 6 shows that 5 of the K items have scale values in the socially desirable category of the equal-appearing interval continuum. These 5 items are scored, according to the K key, only if answered "No" by the subject, that is, if a *desirable* characteristic is *denied* by the subject. This "misdirection" in scoring undoubtedly contributes to the "impurity" of K as a measure of the tendency to give socially desirable responses, as may also the scoring of some of the 8 items falling in the neutral category. I would expect, therefore, that scores on the K scale and those on the SD scale would correlate even higher than the values reported if the 5 K items in the socially desirable category were rescored in accordance with their social desirability scale values, that is, in terms of a "Yes" response rather than a "No" response. Rescoring these items should also tend to raise the correlations between the K scale and the various clinical scales of the MMPI.

6

Social Desirability and Faking

In their discussion of the K scale of the MMPI, Meehl and Hathaway (1946), have observed that one of the most important defects of personality inventories is their susceptibility to "faking," that is, the conscious distortion of scores in terms of response tendencies of the subjects taking the inventories. Equally important, they note, is the susceptibility of inventories to unconscious self-deception and role-playing on the part of subjects who may, in general, be quite honest and sincere in their responses to the personality statements contained in the inventories.

Without concern for the distinction between conscious and unconscious distortion, it may be noted that a subject's responses may be "falsified" in such a way that he obtains either a higher or a lower score on a particular variable than he would if his responses were completely accurate. Thus we may describe a subject as either faking good or faking bad. Faking good refers to the tendency to create a more favorable impression or, in general, the tendency to give socially desirable responses to items in self-description. If a subject fakes good, then we may expect him to obtain a higher score on a scale than he otherwise would, if the variable measured by the scale is itself a socially desirable one, that is, if the keyed responses are socially desirable responses. On scales measuring socially undesirable variables, the tendency to fake good should result in a lower score than would otherwise be obtained by the subject, if the keyed responses are socially undesirable responses.

Faking bad, on the other hand, refers to the tendency to create a more unfavorable impression or, in general, the tendency to give socially undesirable responses to items in self-description. Thus the influence of faking bad on scores on personality scales should be just the opposite of faking good. Faking bad may occur in situations where a subject is under the impression that portraying himself in terms of socially undesirable characteristics may work to his advantage. For example, if an individual hopes that he will be discharged from the army if he portrays himself as psychoneurotic, he may endorse an unusually large number of characteristics (statements) that would, in general, be considered socially undesirable. To fake bad in some situations may be of importance, but it does not seem that this tendency is as prevalent as that to fake good.

Since my interest is in social desirability, or faking good, I shall be concerned only with those studies of fakability in which subjects are expected to give favorable or socially desirable self-descriptions. Many of these studies have been reviewed by Meehl and Hathaway (1946) and by Ellis (1946).

The procedure frequently used in studies of faking is to have subjects take an inventory under standard instructions for self-description and then to obtain a second record from the same subjects under special instructions to fake. In some cases the special instructions have involved telling the subjects to answer the items as they would if they were applicants for a particular job. In others the special instructions have involved telling the subjects to answer the items in such a way as to create a good impression. It is the latter type of study that is of some interest as far as the social desirability variable is concerned.

A study by Rosen (1956), mentioned earlier, is particularly appropriate. He had subjects take a shortened form of the MMPI under standard instructions. The subjects were then told to answer "True" or "False" to the same items on the basis of what they considered desirable characteristics in others. When we examine the scores obtained by the subjects under the two conditions of administration, what should we expect to find?

It seems reasonable to assume that under standard instructions subjects will differ in their tendencies to respond to items in personality inventories in terms of social desirability. If the SD scale does, in fact, measure this tendency, then the distribution of individual differences is such that the median falls toward the high end of the continuum; that is, most of the subjects show the tendency to a rather high degree with a tailing off in the number of subjects toward the low end of the score continuum. In taking a personality inventory under standard instructions, I would assume that the responses of subjects with high SD scores are more influenced by considerations of social desirability than are those of subjects with low SD scores. Then, if the same group of subjects is given the same personality inventory with special instructions to give socially desirable responses, what changes can be expected in their responses to the items in the inventory? We will not be concerned here with the distinction between subtle and obvious items.

If a subject's responses under standard instructions are already primarily influenced by considerations of social desirability, special instructions to attend to social desirability should not result in any marked shifts in his responses. The special instructions, in other words, should be expected to have relatively little influence on the scores of subjects who responded initially in terms of social desirability. On the other hand, subjects whose initial responses to the items under standard instructions were relatively little influenced by social desirability considerations might be expected to show marked shifts in their responses under the special instructions.

Special instructions to fake good, in other words, would not operate in the same manner for all subjects, but would depend, rather, upon the extent to which each subject's responses under standard instructions were already influenced by social desirability considerations. Thus the scores of individuals relatively uninfluenced by desirability considerations on the first administration should, as a result of the special instructions to give desirable responses, shift in the direction of the scores of individuals who on the first administration were already influenced by social desirability considerations. The scores of the latter individuals, however, should change relatively little as a result of the special instructions. The net effect of these differential shifts under special instructions should be to make all scores more homogenous or, in other words, to restrict the range. If this analysis is correct, we would predict relatively low correlations between scores obtained under the two conditions of administration as compared with, let us say, the usual test-retest reliability coefficients.

The fact is that relatively low intercorrelations have been found in terms of the two conditions of administration. This is true in the case of Rosen's (1956) study with the MMPI scales and also in the case of an earlier study by Bernreuter (1933) with the scales of the Bernreuter Personality Inventory.

In Rosen's study, a discrepancy score was obtained for each subject. This score was based upon the number of items answered in one way under standard instructions and in a different way under instructions to give desirable responses. The discrepancy score might thus be considered a measure of the extent to which an individual's responses to items are influenced by the special instructions to give desirable responses. The higher the score, then apparently the greater is the influence of the special instructions.

If my contention that the instructions to give desirable responses operate differentially upon subjects is correct, that is, if the degree of influence depends upon the extent to which responses under standard instructions are influenced by social desirability considerations, we should expect the discrepancy score to be negatively correlated with the score on the SD scale obtained under the standard instructions. Rosen does not report the correlations between the discrepancy score and the SD scale, but he does give the correlation between the discrepancy score and the score on the K scale obtained under the standard instructions. The observed correlation between these two variables was −.60 for males and −.65 for females. In other words, the higher the K score, under standard instructions, the smaller is the number of changes in response under the instructions to give desirable answers.

Rosen interprets high scores on the K scale as indicating "defensiveness" upon the part of the subjects. I would interpret scores on this scale, within the limitations noted earlier, as measures of the tendency to give socially desirable responses in self-description. That Rosen's notion of defensiveness is, in fact, nearly the same as my notion of social desirability is indicated by his statement that "if K can be taken as a measure of defensiveness, then a high correlation (between the discrepancy score and K) can be taken as evidence for the hypothesis that the previously reported correlation—that between self-endorsement and desirability (.87)—is at least in part due to the conscious or unconscious attempt to give good self-impressions" (1956, p. 157). Thus the correlations of −.60 and −.65 between the discrepancy score and the score on the K scale are also in accord with the hypothesis advanced earlier that individuals with high SD (or K) scores should be less influenced by instructions to give desirable responses than those with low SD (or K) scores.

For reasons discussed earlier, I would not take K to be as pure a measure of the tendency to give socially desirable responses in self-description as SD. I would predict, therefore, that the correlation between the discrepancy score and the score on the SD scale would be even higher than that obtained between the discrepancy score and K.

Faking good on personality inventories, without special instructions to do so, I would consider equivalent to the tendency to give socially desirable responses in self-description. It is this tendency, of course, that the SD was designed to measure. A subject may fake good on a personality scale measuring, let us say, dominance and thus distort the meaning of his score with respect to the variable we hope to measure, that is, dominance. It is interesting to consider, however, that, if a subject fakes good on the SD scale, he is, in fact, showing the very tendency we hope to measure with the scale.

The results of studies of faking good have occasionally been interpreted as offering evidence as to whether or not subjects tended to give socially desirable responses under standard instructions. We would, of course, expect mean scores on socially desirable variables to be higher under instructions to fake good than under standard instructions, whereas mean scores on socially undesirable variables should be lower. If the observed differences are in the expected direction, this result in no way rules out the possibility that subjects were giving, in some degree, socially desirable responses under the standard instructions. As Meehl and Hathaway (1946) have stressed, at best the occurrence of shifts in mean scores merely indicates that conscious faking has a greater influence than the faking which may have been taking place under standard instructions.

If no change occurs in scores obtained under standard instructions and under instructions to fake good, this also does not necessarily mean that faking was not taking place under standard instructions. It could equally well be interpreted as meaning that the tendency to give socially desirable responses was influential to such an extent under standard instructions that special instructions to fake good could not in any way increase the tendency. Failure to find shifts in scores under the two conditions of administration, however, would surely seem to be a more unusual result than to observe that the shifts did occur. No matter what the result, however, we can only conclude that studies of faking good have little or no bearing upon the problem of whether or not scores obtained under standard instructions have been distorted by the tendency to give socially desirable responses.

7

The Forced-Choice Inventory

THREE APPROACHES TO the control of social desirability in personality inventories have been suggested. One, following the suggestion of Wiener (1948) and Hanley (1956), is to attempt to develop inventories in which the statements are primarily of the subtle or neutral type with respect to social desirability. Another approach, emphasized by Meehl and Hathaway (1946), involves the use of a scale such as the K or SD scale which, we have reason to believe, measures the tendency of subjects to give socially desirable responses to items in personality inventories. Scores on the K or SD scale can then be used to correct the scores obtained on other inventories for this tendency. A third approach is the one which I used in developing the Personal Preference Schedule (Edwards, 1953*b*).

In this inventory the statements are paired on the basis of their social desirability scale values. The statements appearing in the inventory, for example, were first scaled for social desirability and then paired in terms of their scale values. For each pair of statements the subject is asked to choose that member of the pair that he believes is the more descriptive of himself. The more nearly equivalent we can make the social desirability scale values of the pairs of statements, the more difficult we hope to make the choice of the subject in terms of social desirability alone. The procedure of asking subjects to choose between two or more statements is often referred to as a forced-choice technique. The use of the forced-choice technique in ratings has been described by Sisson (1948) and in the measurement of attitudes by Hammond (1948).

As one might expect, there are some subjects who find that being forced to choose between two statements that are fairly comparable with respect to social desirability scale values is a disagreeable and sometimes frustrating experience. In my research with the PPS, I have upon occasion been maligned by a few such subjects. It is tempting to interpret these expressions of hostility as testimonials to the success with which the factor of social desirability has been controlled in the PPS. More objective evidence on this point, however, is available.

There are 210 different pairs of statements in the PPS. One of the statements in each pair is referred to as the A statement and the other as the B statement. The intraclass correlation between the social desirability scale values of these AB pairs of statements is .85. This correlation indicates that, although the matching of the statements with respect to social desirability scale values is fairly good, it is not perfect. The distribution of the pairs of statements according to their scale separations is such that for 160 or approximately 76 per cent of the 210 pairs the scale separation on the social desirability continuum is within the range .0 to .5 of a scale unit. In the remaining 50 pairs, either the scale value of the A statement exceeds that of the B statement by .5 scale unit, or the scale value of the B statement exceeds that of the A statement by .5 scale unit.

From the original normative group of 1509 subjects a serial random sample of 81 males and 79 females was drawn.* For this sample the proportion endorsing the A statement in each of the 210

* The normative group of 1509 subjects was a national sample of male and female college students obtained in standardizing the PPS. The nature of the normative sample is described in greater detail in the *Manual for the Personal Preference Schedule* (Edwards, 1953*b*).

AB pairs of statements was found. In Figure 7 the probability of an A choice is plotted against the scale separation of the statements, A–B. The product-moment correlation between the probability of an A choice and the magnitude of the scale separation between the A and B statements is .40.

That we would find some degree of relationship between the probability of an A choice and the scale separation of the A and B statements was to be expected for several reasons. In the first place, we know that the pairs of statements are not perfectly equated for social desirability scale values, since the intraclass correlation between these pairs of values is .85 rather than 1.00. In the second place, we know that approximately 50 of the 210 pairs of statements have scale separations greater than .5 unit on the social desirability continuum. I would judge that this amount of scale separation, or perhaps even less, is sufficiently above threshold to permit discrimination. Thus responses to these 50 pairs of statements should be more influenced by considerations of social desirability than the responses to the remaining 160 pairs where the scale separations are less than .5 scale unit. We can see this quite clearly when we compare the points at the extreme right and the extreme left of Figure 7. When the A statement has a markedly higher scale value than the B statement, the number of subjects endorsing the A statement tends to exceed 50 per cent. When the A statement has a markedly lower scale value than the B statement, the number of subjects choosing the A statement tends to be less than 50 per cent. Within the central range, the probability of an A choice bears little or no relationship to the scale separation of the A and B statements.

We must consider also that in the present instance the correlation of .40 between the probability of an A choice and the scale separation of the A and B statements enables us to account for only 16 per cent of the total variance in the probability of an A response in terms of the differences in the scale values of the pairs of statements. On the other hand, when these same statements were administered in the usual "Yes-No" type of personality inventory, the

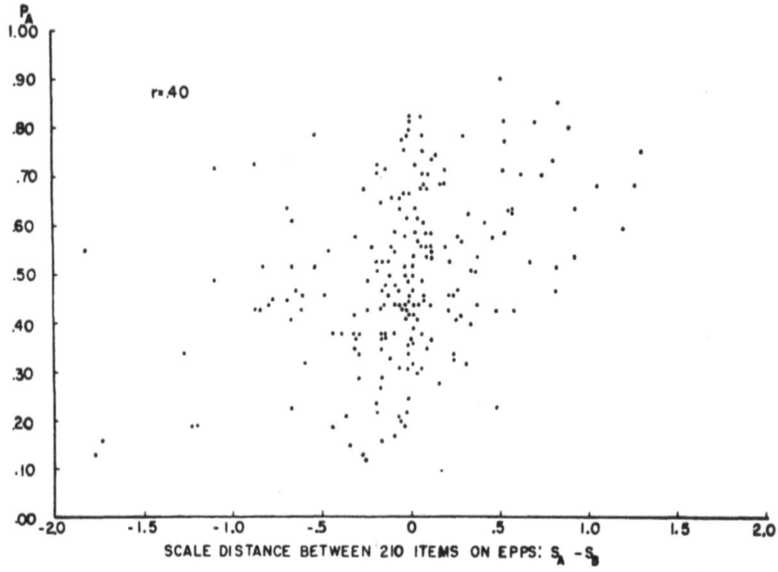

FIG. 7. *Probability of an A response in the AB pairs of statements in the Personal Preference Schedule as related to the social desirability scale separation of the pairs of statements.*

correlation between probability of endorsement and the social desirability scale value was .87 (Edwards, 1953*a*). A correlation of .87 enables us to account for 76 per cent of the total variance in probability of endorsement in terms of the social desirability scale differences of the statements. It is clear that, by pairing the statements in terms of social desirability scale values, a fair degree of control over the tendency to give socially desirable responses is achieved.

Some indication of the stability of the correlation of .40 that I found between probability of an A choice and the scale separation A-B is provided by Wright's (1957) research. He gave the PPS to a sample of 134 college students and found, for this sample, the probability of an A choice for each of the 210 pairs of statements. Using my scale values, the correlation between probability of an A choice and the scale separation of the pairs of statements was .45.

In a repetition of this research with a group of high-school students, Klett (1956) found a correlation of .37 between probability of an A choice and the scale separation of the statements, A–B. This correlation indicates that one could account for 14 per cent of the total variance in probability of endorsement in terms of the scale separations of the statements, and the finding is consistent with the result I obtained with college students. The correlation is, however, based upon the scale separations of the statements in terms of the scale values originally obtained from the judgments of a group of college students. A somewhat higher correlation was obtained between probability of an A choice and scale separation of the statements when the scale separations were based upon the scale values derived from high-school judges. In this instance the correlation was .51, indicating that one could account for 26 per cent of the total variance in probability of endorsement in terms of the social desirability scale differences of the statements.

Additional evidence bearing upon the extent to which the social desirability variable is controlled in the forced-choice inventory is available. Scores on the 79-item and 39-item SD scales, described previously, have been correlated with each of the 15 personality variables of the PPS. Table 7 shows the magnitude of the correlations that have been obtained by three different investigators (Edwards, 1953*b*; Merrill and Heathers, 1956; Crow, 1957) with three different groups of subjects. The correlations shown in the first column are product-moment correlations based upon a college sample of 106 students. Those in the second column are tetrachoric correlations based upon a sample of 155 males tested at a university counseling center. Those in the third column are also tetrachoric correlations and are based upon a sample of 100 Np patients at a VA hospital. Since the K scale, to some extent, also measures the tendency to give socially desirable responses, the correlations of the 15 PPS variables with the K scale for the same samples are also given in the table.

If one compares the magnitude of the correlations shown in Table 7 with those shown in Tables 3 and 5, where the SD scale

TABLE 7

CORRELATIONS BETWEEN THE PPS SCALES AND THE SD AND K SCALES

PPS Scale	*SD Scale*			*K Scale*		
	(1)	(2)	(3)	(1)	(2)	(3)
1. Achievement	.09	—.18	—.22	—.01	—.09	—.06
2. Deference	.09	.20	.52	.03	.07	.25
3. Order	.19	—.04	.12	.16	.05	.03
4. Exhibition	—.08	.28	—.06	—.05	.11	.03
5. Autonomy	—.17	—.04	—.07	—.26	.02	.03
6. Affiliation	—.02	.17	.29	.08	.30	.19
7. Intraception	.06	.15	.15	.16	.23	—.06
8. Succorance	—.32	—.21	—.28	—.25	—.17	—.31
9. Dominance	—.02	.51	—.09	.04	.33	—.19
10. Abasement	—.14	—.46	.03	.08	—.35	—.06
11. Nurturance	—.08	—.13	.16	.08	.15	.19
12. Change	.08	.05	—.10	.05	—.15	.06
13. Endurance	.32	.21	.17	.24	.21	.31
14. Heterosexuality	.07	—.13	—.13	—.15	—.14	—.16
15. Aggression	—.10	—.26	—.15	—.33	—.33	—.19

(1) Edwards (1953*b*): $N = 106$ College Students; 79-item SD scale; r.
(2) Merrill and Heathers (1956): $N = 155$ counseling center males; 39-item SD scale: r_t.
(3) Crow (1957): $N = 100$ VA Np males; 39-item SD scale; r_t.

was correlated with inventories of the "Yes-No" type, it is obvious that the SD scale correlates lower with the variables measured by this forced-choice type of inventory than it does with those measured by the "Yes-No" type of inventory. On the basis of these correlations alone, however, I would not want to conclude that the observed lower correlations of SD with the PPS variables are to be attributed solely to the forced-choice format of the PPS. It is also possible that the variables measured by the PPS are not themselves of such a nature as to be considered either highly socially desirable or undesirable, whereas this would not be true, for example, for the variables measured by the clinical scales of the MMPI. If the variables being measured by the PPS have any relevance to the names assigned to them, however, it does not seem likely that these variables, at least for college students taking the inventory under standard instructions, would be considered neutral with respect to social desirability. Navran and Stauffacher (1954), for example, asked 25 student affiliate nurses at a Veterans Administration hospital to rank the 15 PPS variables in terms of social desirability. The range and distribution of mean ranks assigned to the variables by this group indicated that there was good agreement among them in their judgments of social desirability.

Navran and Stauffacher (1954) also asked the nurses to provide self-descriptions of the 15 PPS variables by having them rank the variables from most to least descriptive. The definitions of the variables given to the nurses were those contained in the *Manual for the Personal Preference Schedule* (Edwards, 1593*b*). The rank-order correlation between the mean ranks assigned the variables in self-description and in social desirability was .90. This, of course, is what we would expect to find in terms of our previous discussion of the relationship between probability of endorsement of personality statements and their social desirability scale values. In obtaining the self-descriptive rankings, no attempt is made to control for the social desirability variable. This is not the case, however, in the PPS itself. There an attempt is made to minimize social desirability for the 15 variables. We should expect to find, therefore, that the mean ranks assigned the variables in social desirability have little or no relation to the mean scores on the variables obtained from actual PPS test records. Navran and Stauffacher report that this is so. They had previously given the nurses the PPS and were thus able to obtain a mean score for the group on each variable based upon their responses in the test situation. The rank-order correlation between these mean scores and the mean ranks assigned the variables in social desirability was .01.

A study by Kelleher (1957) also relates to the control of social desirability in the PPS. Kelleher gave the PPS and a 40-item SD scale to a group of 101 college males and a group of 101 college females.* For each group of subjects he computed point-biserial correlations between scores on the SD scale and each of the 210 pairs of statements in the PPS. It was his hope that he might find a sufficient number of items within the PPS which would correlate with scores on the SD scale so that a measure of the tendency to give socially desirable responses internal to the PPS could be developed.

Table 8 gives the distribution of the 210 point-biserial correlation coefficients for the group of males and for the group of females. It is apparent that relatively few of the items have correlations of any magnitude with scores on the SD scale.

TABLE 8

DISTRIBUTIONS OF 210 POINT-BISERIAL CORRELATIONS BETWEEN SCORES ON THE SD SCALE AND RESPONSES TO ITEMS IN THE PPS AS OBTAINED FROM A GROUP OF 101 FEMALES AND A GROUP OF 101 MALES[1]

Point-Biserial *r's*	*Females* *f*	*Males* *f*
.30 to .39	2	2
.20 to .29	12	12
.10 to .19	45	32
.00 to .09	59	64
—.00 to .09	49	61
—.10 to .19	27	28
—.20 to .29	12	10
—.30 to .39	3	1
—.40 to .49	1	

[1] Kelleher (1957).

* The SD scale used by Kelleher consisted of the 39-item SD scale plus one additional item, keyed "True," that is not contained in the MMPI. There is no reason to believe that the inclusion of this one additional item would in any way change the nature of the results he would have found if it had been omitted.

Kelleher also obtained a score for each of the subjects in his two groups which was based upon the number of times the subject chose the statement with the higher social desirability scale value in each of the pairs of statements in the PPS. The correlations between these scores and scores on the SD scale were .02 for the 101 females and .17 for the 101 males.

There is additional evidence to indicate that, when one pairs statements on the basis of social desirability scale values, the tendency of subjects to give socially desirable responses is minimized. Consider for a moment the fact that, when we find the intercorrelations between scores on various personality inventories of the "Yes-No" type, it is not at all unusual to find that the correlations obtained are of considerable magnitude. This is true even when the variables which the different inventories are supposed to measure are believed to be independent.

If we assume that each of the scales, in addition to the variable that it is believed to measure, has a substantial loading on a factor of social desirability common to all the scales, the magnitude of the intercorrelations between scales can be accounted for. If it were possible to minimize the operation of the social desirability variable in the personality domain, one might expect relatively lower intercorrelations between various personality measures. As pointed out previously, an attempt has been made to do this in the PPS by pairing statements in terms of their social desirability scale values.

If the approach used in developing the scales in this inventory has been successful in minimizing the social desirability variable, one might expect to find the intercorrelations of the variables to be of relatively small magnitude. Table 9 gives the distribution of the 105 intercorrelations, based upon the scores of the normative group of 1509 college students used in standardizing the schedule (Edwards, 1953*b*). Of the 105 intercorrelations, the highest is .46 between Affiliation and Nurturance, and the next highest is −.36 between Autonomy and Nurturance. The remaining 103 intercorrelations are indeed quite low. The intercorrelations of these variables

TABLE 9

DISTRIBUTION OF THE 105 INTERCORRELATIONS BETWEEN THE 15 VARIABLES OF THE PPS[1]

Numerical Values	*Positive Correlations*	*Negative Correlations*
	f	*f*
.45 to .49	1	
.40 to .44		
.35 to .39		1
.30 to .34	1	9
.25 to .29	2	7
.20 to .24	3	11
.15 to .19	5	15
.10 to .14	7	12
.05 to .09	13	9
.00 to .04	5	4

[1] Edwards (1953*b*).

have now been obtained by four different investigators (Edwards, 1953*b*; Klett, 1956; Merrill and Heathers, 1956; Strother and Schaie, 1955) with four different samples and with essentially the same results as those shown in Table 9.

It might be argued, of course, that the reason the relatively low intercorrelations are found is that each of the variables being measured is itself neutral with respect to social desirability. In view of evidence provided by Navran and Stauffacher (1954), this does not seem to be the case. They found that their subjects agreed quite well in their rankings of the social desirability of the 15 variables measured by the PPS. If all the variables were essentially neutral with respect to social desirability, we would expect little agreement among the ranks assigned by the different judges, with the result that each variable would have an average rank close to 8.0. The average ranks actually obtained, on the other hand, ranged from 3.5 to 14.3, indicating that there are judged differences in the social desirability of the 15 variables. It does not appear, therefore, that we could account for the relatively low intercorrelations among the 15 variables on the basis of the argument that they are neutral with respect to social desirability.

The variety of evidence presented in this chapter would seem to indicate that pairing statements with comparable social desirability scale values has much to offer in the way of developing personality measures free from the tendency of subjects to give socially desirable responses. This does not mean, however, that personality measures of the kind described cannot and will not be subject to faking under special conditions of administrations.

In the research cited in this chapter, for example, the PPS was administered under conditions where I would assume that general cultural norms of social desirability were involved. By this I mean that the conditions of administration were such that the social desirability scale values of the pairs of statements could be expected to be much the same as they were for the original judging group from which they were derived. In terms of the instructions given to the original judging group, I would assume that their judgments were based upon notions of general cultural norms of social desirability applicable to people in general and not upon special norms of social desirability which might be applicable to particular selected groups of individuals. As long as the conditions of administration involve general cultural norms of social desirability, I would expect responses to the pairs of statements to be relatively uninfluenced by the social desirability variable.

Suppose, however, that the original judging group had been asked to make their judgments in terms of specific norms of social desirability. For example, suppose that they had been asked to judge each statement in terms of whether they considered the trait a desirable or an undesirable one in physicians. These judging instructions might have resulted in a different set of social desirability scale values than the ones I obtained under the more general instructions. This would be true if the personality characteristics regarded as desirable in physicians differed in any significant way from those regarded as desirable in people in general. A similar argument could be made with reference to any other special group for which the norms of social desirability might differ from the general cultural norms.

Now, let us assume that the PPS is to be administered to a group of applicants for admission to a medical school. Let us assume also that the personality traits measured by the inventory and considered desirable for success in the medical profession are different from the personality traits considered desirable in the general population. This is to say, in other words, that the social desirability scale values for the statements in the inventory would differ from those of the general population if scaled for social desirability in terms of the traits believed to be desirable in physicians. Thus two statements that may be relatively equal as far as social desirability is concerned with respect to the general cultural norms would no longer be equated with respect to the norms applicable to this special group. If the medical school applicants are motivated to create a good impression in terms of the norms of social desirability of physicians, and if they can perceive differences in the social desirability scale values of the pairs of statements in terms of these norms, we may expect their responses to be influenced by these circumstances.

For example, if the social desirability scale values of the statements relating to Achievement were much higher when scaled for social desirability in terms of the norms for physicians than when scaled in terms of the norms for the general population, then all the pairs of statements in the PPS in which one of the members of the pair is a statement relating to Achievement would be much more widely separated in terms of social desirability scale values than they would be for the general population which determined the original pairing. When choosing between these pairs of statements, we might expect the choices of medical school applicants to be influenced in the direction of the statements they consider more socially desirable. Thus we would expect the medical school applicants to obtain a much higher mean on the Achievement variable than was obtained for the original standardization group.

Under the conditions described, the interpretation to be placed on a high (or low) score for a particular variable of the PPS is subject to many of the same difficulties we encountered in our discussion of scores on inventories of the "Yes-No" type. Nor do I see any easy solution to the difficulties. Can we conclude that the observed difference in the mean of the scale for the medical applicants is a function of what the group believes to be socially desirable, or does it reflect a difference in the degree to which the variable characterizes the group? I agree with Klett (1957) that we do not know. "It is," he states, "just as obvious that judgments of what is socially desirable are in part a function of the dominant traits of the judging group as it is that probability of endorsement of an item is a function of the social desirability scale value of the item. The two are inextricably confounded."

Suppose, however, that it could be shown that the social desirability scale values of the statements in the scale on which the mean difference is observed are the same when judged in the context of norms of social desirability appropriate to the two groups. Then we would have some confidence that the difference was not the result of different social desirability norms.

The important point is that general cultural norms of social desirability provide only a kind of "standard," and that we must still be concerned with potential deviations of special norms from this standard. It is obvious that much research remains to be done in this area.

8

Social Desirability in Q-Technique

IN Q-TECHNIQUE STUDIES, as described by Stephenson (1953), subjects are frequently asked to describe themselves by sorting personality statements into a set of successive categories or intervals, ranging from the least descriptive to the most descriptive. The number of statements to be placed in each interval is fixed by the experimenter so that the resulting frequency distribution is somewhat normal in form. Weights or scores are assigned to each of the successive intervals and consequently to the statements within the interval. If 11 intervals are used, for example, the statements placed in the least descriptive category would be given weights of 1 and those in the most descriptive category weights of 11, the other 9 intervals being assigned the successive integers between 1 and 11.

Stephenson has described the use of "structured" and "unstructured" samples of statements in Q-technique. By an unstructured sample he means a set of statements which have not been subdivided in any way by the experimenter into smaller subsets. Thus a set of items in a personality inventory, designed to yield but a single score, might be taken as an example of an unstructured sample. By a structured sample Stephenson means that we have at least two kinds of items with an equal number of each kind. For example, if we had 50 items designed to measure dominance and 50 items designed to measure submission, we would have the simplest kind of structured sample.

More complex structured samples of statements may be constructed in terms of a factorial design. For example, a set of 96 statements might be first subdivided into sets of 48 items each, according to whether the items are believed to measure "dependency" or "independency." Assume also that within each set of 48 items we can form two sets of 24 items each, according to whether the items are believed to measure "behavior" or "feelings." Such a set of items would correspond, in analysis of variance terms, to a 2×2 factorial design.

For either structured or unstructured samples of items we have a score for each of the statements for each of the subjects involved. For unstructured samples, the analysis of the data is often carried out by correlating the scores assigned to the items for all possible pairs of subjects and then factoring the obtained correlation matrix. For structured samples, correlations between subjects can also be obtained and the resulting matrix factored. Structured samples also permit, however, an analysis of variance of the scores obtained from each single subject.

It is probably safe to assume that, for most sets of statements relating to personality variables, the statements will differ in degree of judged social desirability. On the basis of the evidence cited previously in connection with personality inventories, it seems likely that there should be a tendency for subjects working under the instructions given in a Q-technique study to regard those items with high social desirability scale values as most characteristic of themselves. These items, then, in general, will be assigned to the higher weights, that is, the 11's, 10's, and 9's. Items with lower social desirability scale values will, in general, be placed in the least descriptive categories and consequently will receive the lower weights, that is, the 1's, 2's, and 3's.

A study designed to test this hypothesis has been reported (Edwards, 1955). Social desirability scale values, as determined by the method of successive intervals, were available for 135 items used in developing the PPS. Q-sorts were made with these statements by 50 male and 50 female students at the University of Washington and the University of Oregon. The subjects sorted the statements into 11 categories with frequencies of 5, 7, 8, 14, 20, 27, 20, 14, 8, 7, and 5 statements in the successive categories. A weight of 11 was assigned to the statements in the most descriptive category and a weight of 1 to those in the least descriptive, the other integers between 1 and 11 being assigned to the statements in the categories between the the two extremes.

For each group of subjects the mean value assigned to each statement in the Q-sorts was found. These mean weights were then related to the corresponding social desirability scale values of the statements. Figure 8 shows the plot for the males and Figure 9 the plot for the females. It is clear that in both figures the mean weight assigned to the statement in the Q-sorts is related to the social desirability scale value of the statement. The product-moment correlation between these two variables for the group of males is .84, and for the group of females it is .87. The correlations are of approximately the same magnitude as those reported previously between probability of endorsement of a personality statement and social desirability scale value of the statement.

It is not necessary to have a large number of subjects to find the relationship between the mean Q-values and social desirability scale values shown in Figures 8 and 9. The correlations, for example, would have been almost the same as those reported if but 10 subjects had been used in each group rather than 50. This conclusion has been confirmed by Kenny (1956) with a different set of personality statements. Using Zimmer's (1954) traits, Kenny asked 8 subjects to do Q-sorts under standard instructions to provide self-descriptions. The same subjects also sorted the statements according to their judgments of the social desirability of the traits. The average

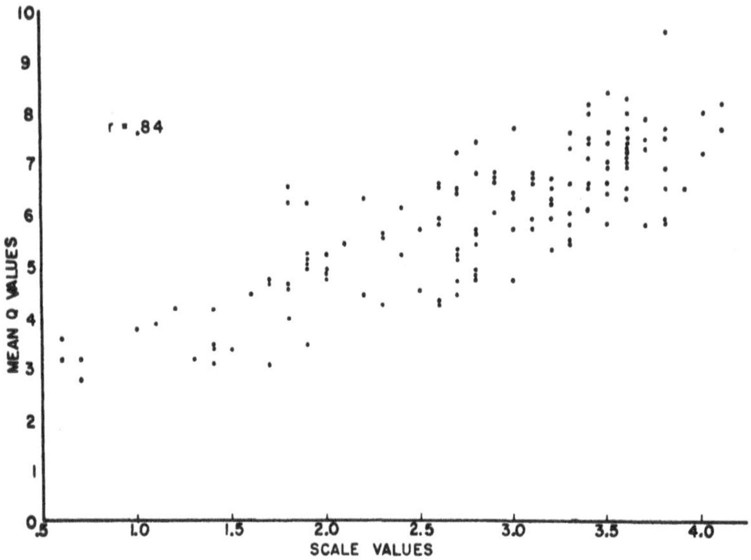

Fig. 8. *Mean value of a statement in Q-sorts from 50 males as related to the social desirability scale value of the statement.*

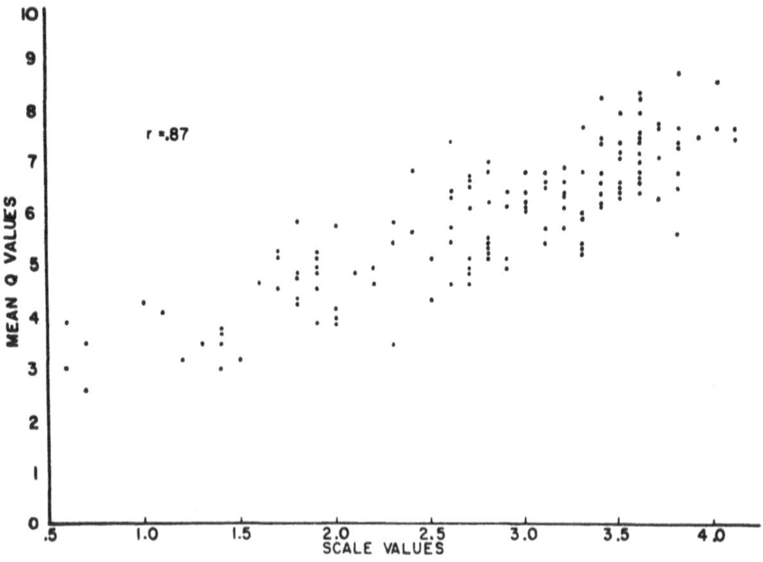

Fig. 9. *Mean value of a statement in Q-sorts from 50 females as related to the social desirability scale value of the statement.*

score assigned to each statement was found for the group of 8 subjects for both sorts. The correlation between the mean values of the statements under instructions for self-description and when the subjects were asked to judge the social desirability of the same statements was .66.

If we consider the self-descriptive Q-sorts of individuals rather than the average, we find that for 7 of the 8 subjects the correlations of self-sorts and the group sort for social desirability are positive and statistically significant.

Results obtained by Taylor (1955) also bear upon the operation of the social desirability variable in Q-sorts. Taylor used a total of 120 items, of which 60 are described as "positive" and 60 as "negative." It would appear safe to assume that the 60 positive items would, in general, have higher social desirability scale values than the 60 negative items. These 120 statements were Q-sorted by 120 subjects who gave self-descriptions in terms of 11 categories. The number of statements placed in each of the successive categories was: 6, 9, 11, 12, 14, 16, 14, 12, 11, 9, and 6. The six statements in the category "most like me" were assigned weights of 11 and the six in the category "least like me" were assigned weights of 1. Statements in the categories between these two extremes were assigned the successive integers between 1 and 11.

If a subject gave equal importance to the positive and negative statements in self-description, the expected score or sum of weights for the positive statements would be 360, as it would be also for the negative statements. Taylor found, however, that 105 of the 120 subjects had scores on the positive statements which exceeded 360. The mean score for all 120 subjects was 421.25. This mean is of particular interest in view of the fact that the *maximum* score that could possibly be obtained for the 60 positive statements is 497.

Taylor also had 7 of his subjects repeat their self-descriptions in terms of the Q-sort twice a day for five consecutive days. The mean score on the first sorting for the 60 positive statements for this group was 433.00, and for the last sort it was 455.86. It would seem, therefore, that for these subjects increased experience with the statements resulted in an accentuation of the tendency to describe themselves primarily in terms of the positive or socially desirable statements. Something similar to this effect has been observed by Neprash (1936) in the case of successive administrations of a personality inventory.

Still further evidence is available on the manner in which social desirability operates in Q-sorts. Kogan, Quinn, Ax, and Ripley (1957) constructed a Q-sort consisting of statements believed to relate to 25 personality variables. Each variable was represented by several statements in the Q-sort, and, instead of dealing with the individual statements, they analyzed their data in terms of the scores for each of the 25 variables.

A small group of clinical psychologists and psychiatrists sorted the statements following a quasi-normal distribution in terms of social desirability. An average weight was obtained from these sorts to represent the social desirability scale values of each of the 25 variables. A second Q-sort was also obtained from the same group of judges under the instructions to sort the statements in terms of sickness-health. These sorts provided an average value for each of the 25 variables with respect to the dimension of sickness-health.

When the sickness and health values of the 25 variables were correlated with the social desirability values, the product-moment correlation was found to be .89. In terms of the 25 variables represented in this Q-sort, we might conclude that the dimension of sickness-health is much the same as the dimension of social desirability-undesirability.

Let us now see what happens when this same Q-sort is used for purposes of self-description and for assessing others. Two groups of subjects are involved. One group consisted of 24 male patients, diagnosed as psychoneurotic, at a VA hospital. The control group consisted of 24 male college students who were paid to participate in the study. Each subject in the two groups made a self-assessment with the Q-sort. The subjects in both groups were then put through an hour-long stress interview conducted by a psychiatrist. Upon completion of the stress interview, the psychiatrist described each subject in terms of the Q-sort. A third Q-sort assessment was made for each subject by another psychiatrist upon the basis of case history reports, a psychiatric interview, and other information available to him.

For each group of subjects the mean Q-score was obtained for each of the 25 personality variables for each of the three assessments, and these means were correlated with the social desirability and sickness-health values for the variables. Table 10 shows these correlations. It is clear that the mean scores for both patient and control groups are substantially related to the mean scores for sickness-health and also for social desirability. The average self-sort for the patient group is, however, somewhat less related to social desirability than that for the control group. Note also the negative correlations between the psychiatrists' assessments and social desirability for the patient group. The patients are described primarily in terms of variables that are regarded as socially undesirable or as indicating sickness, when assessed by the psychiatrists.

TABLE 10

CORRELATIONS BETWEEN MEANS OF Q-SORT VARIABLES AND SOCIAL DESIRABILITY AND SICKNESS-HEALTH[1]

	PATIENTS		CONTROLS	
	Soc. Des.	*Sick-Health*	*Soc. Des.*	*Sick-Health*
Self-sort	.67	.59	.85	.90
Stress psychiatrist	—.45	—.53	.76	.81
Work-up psychiatrist	—.54	—.58	.53	.65
N	24		24	

[1] Kogan, Ax, Quinn, and Ripley (1957).

Our interpretation of the correlations shown in Table 10 is, unfortunately, complicated by the fact that the assessors were aware of whether each subject was a member of the patient or control group. It is of interest to speculate, however, upon the relationship between clinical notions of disturbed, sick, psychoneurotic, or psychotic personalities and an operationally defined conception of the socially undesirable personality. Perhaps varying degrees of mental illness could be defined in terms of the social desirability continuum. We may recall that the psychotic factor, as defined in terms of various MMPI scales, was much the same as the social desirability factor.

If we wish to minimize the social desirability variable in Q-technique studies, one way in which this might be accomplished would be to include in the Q-sort only those statements that have comparable social desirability scale values. If all statements have equivalent social desirability scale values, the placement of the statements in the successive categories in self-description should be free of the tendency to describe oneself primarily in terms of desirable characteristics.

Another possible solution, for structured samples, would be to construct a Q-sort in which the social desirability scale values of the statements are balanced with respect to the variable of primary interest. This procedure, although not controlling for social desirability, would at least enable the investigator to determine which subjects were most influenced by the tendency to describe themselves in terms of socially desirable statements.

Consider, for example, a Q-sort developed by Fordyce (1953) and Lamphere (1953). They were interested in selecting a group of statements designed to measure "dependency" and another group designed to measure "independency." By putting together in a single set an equal number of dependency and independency statements, they hoped to be able to determine whether subjects, in Q-descriptions, would characterize themselves primarily as dependent or independent. Preliminary investigation indicated, however, that the statements relating to independency tended, in general, to be judged as more socially desirable than the statements relating to dependency.

We might assume that, in the population of statements relating to dependency and independency, the distributions of social desirability scale values are as shown in Figure 10. Disregarding social desirability scale values, a sample of n_1 statements is taken to represent dependency and another sample of n_2 statements is taken to represent independency. Subjects are now asked to described themselves in terms of the $N = n_1 + n_2$ statements.

We now apply analysis of variance techniques to the Q-sorts of the individual subjects. If a subject has a mean on the dependency items that is significantly greater than the mean on the independency items, we have some assurance that his description has been made primarily in terms of the dependency variable rather than the social desirability variable. Our assurance is based upon the fact that, in general, the dependency items have lower social desirability scale values than do the independency items.

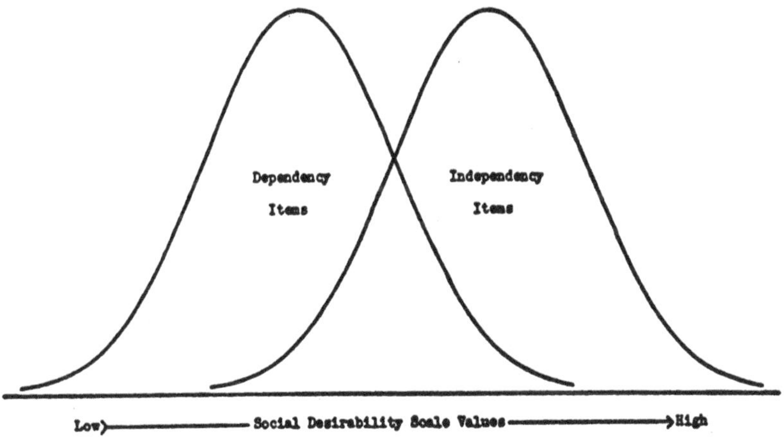

FIG. 10. *Theoretical distributions of social desirability scale values of statements relating to dependency and independency. Source: Edwards and Horst (1953).*

On the other hand, if a subject has a significantly higher mean on the independency items than on the dependency items, we would not know whether this was the result of a strong trait of independency, the result of a tendency to portray oneself as socially desirable, or the result of both variables. In analysis of variance terms, social desirability and independency are completely confounded.

Now consider a structured sample where social desirability has been balanced with respect to the variable of primary interest. We assume now that social desirability scale values have been obtained for the items and that for each of the items in the independency set we have a corresponding item in the dependency set of approximately the same social desirability scale value. We will then have distributions of social desirability scale values in the two sets of items that are comparable. We may arbitrarily classify those items, regardless of the dependency-independency classification, that are above the median in terms of social desirability scale values as "socially desirable" items and those that are below the median as "socially undesirable" items. We thus have, in analysis of variance terms, a 2×2 factorial design incorporated into the sample of items.

Subjects are now asked to describe themselves in terms of a Q-sort with this set of items. The analysis of variance of the Q-sorts for the individual subjects would take the following form:

Source of Variation	*df*
(a) Dependency-independency	1
(b) Social desirability-undesirability	1
(c) Interaction (a) × (b)	1
(d) Replication (error)	N - 4

It is clear from the above summary of the analysis of variance that differentiation of the dependency-independency effect is possible. We also can determine whether a subject describes himself primarily in terms of the social desirability-undesirability variable rather than in terms of the dependency-independency variable. In this 2×2 factorial design, social desirability is no longer confounded with independency.

With social desirability balanced in a structured sample of personality statements, the interpretation of either the analysis of variance of the Q-sorts or of the factors obtained from the correlation matrix is much clearer than it would be if social desirability were not balanced and operated in such a way as to be related to one of the major trait classifications of the items.

9

Implications for Personality Assessment and Research

WE HAVE FOUND that the probability of endorsement of a statement in a personality inventory of the "Yes-No" form or in a Q-sort tends to be positively correlated with the social desirability scale value of the statement. This finding would seem to indicate that in interpreting responses of subjects to items in personality inventories or Q-sorts, some consideration should be given to the social desirability scale values of the items. Since the relationship has been found to hold in terms of both responses to items in personality inventories *and* Q-sorts, it will be convenient in the following discussion to refer only to personality inventories without the necessity of adding "or Q-sorts" each time personality inventories are mentioned. It will be assumed that the discussion is equally pertinent to Q-sorts.

As I have pointed out elsewhere (1953*a*), it is possible that the traits or items which are judged socially desirable are those that are fairly common or dominant among the members of a group. If a characteristic is prevalent or dominant in a group, it will perhaps be judged desirable. If this is the case, we might expect statements relating to desirable traits to be endorsed more frequently than those relating to undesirable traits.

It is also possible that the trait indicated by a statement with a high social desirability scale value is not prevalent or dominant in a group, but that the subject responding to the statement is trying, consciously or unconsciously, to give a good impression. He may therefore respond to the statements in such a way as to attribute to himself more of the socially desirable traits and fewer of the socially undesirable traits than he would if his personality were evaluated in terms of some other criterion. This would also account for the relationship found between probability of endorsement and social desirability scale value.

Under any circumstances, if a statement has a high social desirability scale value and if a subject endorses it in self-description, our interpretation of his response is complicated. We have no way of knowing, for example, whether the statement is, in fact, descriptive of the subject or whether he simply says that it is because he regards it as a socially desirable characteristic. Similarly, if a subject fails to endorse a statement with a low social desirability scale value, he may do so because the statement is not, in fact, descriptive of him, or because he does not choose to acknowledge what he may regard as a socially undesirable characterization.

Comparable difficulties are encountered in attempting to interpret scores on personality inventories or Q-sorts, based upon responses to a group of items. Suppose, for example, that an inventory was developed to measure some trait or variable that we might label "neuroticism." If the signs and symptoms of neuroticism are themselves socially undesirable, as they seem likely to be, we might expect that the statements included in the inventory would be those that would have socially undesirable scale values, with the result that the keyed responses would correspond to socially undesirable responses. It is not too difficult to predict that the score distribution on this inventory would be positively skewed, that is, relatively few high scores would be observed.

On the other hand, if the variable measured by the inventory was itself a socially desirable variable, such as "cooperativeness," we might expect the statements included in the inventory to be primarily those with high social desirability scale values with the keyed responses corresponding to socially desirable responses. In this instance, we would predict that the resulting score distribution on the inventory would be negatively skewed, that is, relatively few low scores would be observed.

To take a specific case, consider the Taylor Manifest Anxiety Scale (1953). Anxiety would probably be judged a socially undesirable trait, and we might guess that the items included in the scale would be primarily those with socially undesirable scale values. For these items we would expect the keyed response to be the socially undesirable response. To obtain a high score on this scale, therefore, it would be necessary to endorse statements that would be judged socially undesirable, that is, to give many socially undesirable responses. It is, we might add, a well-known fact that the observed score distributions on the Taylor scale are positively skewed, as we would expect them to be from our analysis.

A number of studies have used the Taylor scale to select subjects with high and low anxiety, that is, with high and low scores on the scale. Certain hypotheses are entertained concerning the differences to be expected in the behavior of these two groups in an experimental setting. It has been found, for example, that nonanxious subjects, on the average, make fewer errors and require fewer trials to a criterion of learning than do anxious subjects. A great deal of impressive learning theory and speculation has been brought to bear upon this and related findings (Child, 1954; Farber and Spence, 1953; Lucas, 1952; Montague, 1953; Taylor and Spence, 1952). It is worth considering whether this result could not also be accounted for in terms of the social desirability variable.

Let us assume that the two groups selected on the basis of their scores on the Taylor scale differ not with respect to anxiety, but rather with respect to their tendencies to give socially desirable responses to the items in the scale. We have already speculated that, in order to obtain a high score on this scale, a subject must endorse statements that would be judged socially undesirable. An examination of the items in the Taylor scale indicates that, if a subject is to obtain a high score, he must be willing to acknowledge, among other things, that he is lacking in self-confidence, that he cries easily, that he is easily embarrassed, that he is unhappy most of the time, and that at times he thinks he is no good at all. I think we would have to agree that, if a subject attributes these characteristics to himself in self-description, he is acknowledging characteristics that would probably be judged socially undesirable in people in general. High scores on the Taylor scale can only be obtained by endorsing these and other socially undesirable characteristics. Low scores, on the other hand, can be obtained by anyone who simply responds to the items by denial of socially undesirable characteristics. That this is indeed the case is demonstrated by Rosen's (1956) finding that, under instructions to give desirable responses, his subjects obtained a mean score of about 1.0 on the Taylor scale, that is, the average number of *keyed* responses given was about one per subject.

As shown in Table 3, a correlation of −.84 was found between the Taylor scale and the 39-item SD scale, and a correlation of −.60 between the Taylor scale and the 79-item SD scale.* These negative correlations indicate that subjects who obtain low scores on the Taylor scale are those who, in general, would obtain high scores on the SD scale. Scores on the SD scale, it will be recalled, are based upon the frequency with which a subject has given socially desirable responses to the items in the scale.

* To determine the extent to which the negative correlation between scores on the 39-item SD scale and the Anxiety scale could be accounted for in terms of the overlapping 22 items which are scored in the opposite direction, I scored a sample of 155 MMPI records for the Anxiety scale and for the 17 items in the SD scale which do not appear in the Anxiety scale. The correlation between scores based on the 17-item SD scale and the Anxiety scale was −.55. The BSD and the TSD scales, described earlier, both correlated −.65 with the Anxiety scale. It does not appear, therefore, that we can account for the rather high negative correlation between the SD scale and the Anxiety scale merely in terms of the item overlap between the two scales.

I believe it possible, therefore, to describe the low group on the Taylor scale as those who desire to make a good impression on others and the high group as those who are less interested in what others may think of them. I would predict that the group desiring to make a good impression on the Taylor scale, that is to say, those with low scores, might also desire to make a good impression in terms of their performance on the learning task. They are, in other words, perhaps more highly motivated by the desire to "look good," not only in their responses to the Taylor scale, but also in their performance in the learning situation itself. Surely, to be able to learn fast is, in our society, a socially desirable characteristic. If a subject has a strong tendency to give socially desirable responses in self-description, is it unreasonable to believe that he may also reveal this tendency in his behavior in a learning situation where he is aware of what would be considered socially desirable, namely to learn fast, to do his best? The high group, on the other hand, being less interested in making a good impression, showing less of a tendency to give socially desirable responses in self-description, caring less about how others may value them, does not have equal motivation with the low group in the learning situation.

A series of experiments by Mandler and Sarason (1952) and Sarason, Mandler, and Craighill (1952) are also, I believe, in accord with this interpretation. In these studies a scale designed to measure "test-taking anxiety," rather than the Taylor scale, was used to select high and low groups. The performance of these groups under varying experimental conditions was then investigated. The correlation between the "test-taking anxiety" scale and the SD scale is not known, but the results of these studies appear to me, in general, to be consistent with the characterization of the high and low anxiety groups on the Taylor scale in terms of the social desirability variable.

Now we shall shift positions for a moment. Assume that high scores on the Taylor scale do indicate anxiety and/or the tendency to acknowledge socially undesirable characteristics. Low scores, on the other hand, may indicate the absence of anxiety and/or the tendency to defend against self-criticism by the denial of socially undesirable characteristics.

May not the tendency to defend against self-criticism, if it exists, itself be indicative of anxiety? It would seem reasonable that a person might be characterized as anxious if he is overly concerned about the impression he makes on others. If this concern, in turn, is reflected in the manner in which he responds to the items in the Taylor scale, that is, if he gives only socially desirable responses to the items, he will, of necessity, obtain a low score. The results of Rosen's (1956) study, cited earlier, establish this conclusion only too well. His subjects, under instructions to give socially desirable responses, on the average, gave only about one keyed response per subject. Thus it is possible that a group of low scorers, described as nonanxious because of their low scores on the Taylor scale, may include any number of subjects who are, in reality, highly anxious in the sense described.

If the Taylor scale is measuring primarily anxiety, then I would have much more confidence in the characterization of the high group as anxious than I would in the characterization of the low group as nonanxious. It would seem to me that the low group should be much more heterogeneous with respect to anxiety than the range of their scores may indicate.

I selected the Taylor scale for discussion in terms of the social desirability variable because it is a fairly well-known personality inventory and because it has been rather widely used in a research setting. The points I have tried to make with respect to the Taylor scale, however, would apply equally well to other personality inventories where the trait or variable being measured can itself be described as socially desirable or undesirable and where we have reason to believe that the scores may reflect the tendency to acknowledge socially desirable characteristics and the denial of socially undesirable characteristics. The same argument would also apply to scores based upon Q-sorts.

If the scores on any given personality inventory have a substantial proportion of their variance in common with the social desirability variable, under what conditions can we expect the scores on the inventory to be related to other behavior of interest? It seems most reasonable to believe that differences in the behavior of high and low scoring groups will be found in those situations where the behavior under study has itself a large proportion of its variance in common with the social desirability variable. For reasons mentioned earlier, learning or other kinds of behavior which may be influenced by motivation to look good would seem to qualify.

If high and low groups are selected in terms of scores on some personality inventory and if the scores on the inventory are also highly correlated with scores on the SD scale, then any differences in the behavior of the two groups in an experimental setting are subject to two possible explanations. The differences may be the result of the personality variable named and supposedly measured by the personality inventory. They may also be the result of the social desirability variable rather than the personality variable named by the inventory.

Bibliography

Bibliography

ALLPORT, G. W., and ODBERT, H. S. Trait-names, a psychological study. *Psychol. Mongr.*, 1936, 47, No. 1.

BERNREUTER, R. G. Validity of the personality inventory. *Person. J.*, 1933, 11, 383–386.

BLUM, G. S. An experimental reunion of psychoanalytic theory with vigilance and defense. *J. abnorm. soc. Psychol.*, 1954, 49, 94–98.

———. Perceptual defense revisited. *J. abnorm. soc. Psychol.*, 1955, 51, 24–29.

CHILD, I. L. Personality. In C. P. Stone (Ed.), *Annual review of psychology*. Stanford, Calif.: Annual Reviews, 1954. Pp. 149–170.

COOK, W., and MEDLEY, D. M. Proposed hostility and pharasaic-virtue scales for the MMPI. *J. appl. Psychol.*, 1954, 38, 414–418.

CRONBACH, L. J. Response sets and test validity. *Educ. Psychol. Measmt.*, 1946, 6, 475–494.

———. Further evidence on response sets and test design. *Educ. Psychol. Measmt.*, 1950, 10, 3–31.

CRONBACH, L. J., and MEEHL, P. E. Construct validity in psychological tests. *Psychol. Bull.*, 1955, 52, 281–302.

CROW, W. R. Relationships between Edwards PPS and the MMPI. Unpublished master's thesis, Univ. of Washington, 1957.

DRAKE, L. E. A social I. E. scale for the MMPI. *J. appl. Psychol.*, 1946, 30, 51–54.

EDWARDS, A. L. The relationship between the judged desirability of a trait and the probability that the trait will be endorsed. *J. appl. Psychol.*, 1953*a*, 37, 90–93.

———. *Manual for the Edwards Personal Preference Schedule.* New York: Psychol. Corp., 1953*b*.

Edwards, A. L. Social desirability and Q sorts. *J. consult. Psychol.*, 1955, 19, 462.

———. *Techniques of attitude scale construction.* New York: Appleton-Century, 1957.

———. Social desirability and probability of endorsement of items in the Interpersonal Check List. *J. abnorm. soc. Psychol.*, 1958, in press.

Edwards, A. L., and Horst, P. Social desirability as a variable in Q technique studies. *Educ. psychol. Measmt.*, 1953, 13, 620–625.

Ellis, A. The validity of personality questionnaires. *Psychol. Bull.*, 1946, 43, 385–440.

Employee Relations Department. *Employee relations research in Standard Oil Company (New Jersey) and Affiliates.* Vol. 1. New York: Standard Oil Company, 1955.

Eysenck, H. J. *The scientific study of personality.* London: Routledge and Kegan Paul Ltd., 1952.

Farber, I. E., and Spence, K. W. Complex learning and conditioning as a function of anxiety. *J. exp. Psychol.*, 1953, 45, 120–125.

Ferguson, L. W. *Personality measurement.* New York: McGraw-Hill, 1952.

Fordyce, W. E. Applications of a scale of dependency to concepts of self, ideal-self, mother and father. Unpublished doctor's dissertation, Univ. of Washington, 1953.

———. Social desirability in the MMPI. *J. consult. Psychol.*, 1956, 20, 171–175.

Fordyce, W. E., and Rozynko, V. The correlations between the SD scale and the subtle and obvious scales of the MMPI. Personal communication, 1957.

Fujita, B. An investigation of the applicability of the PPS to a cultural subgroup. Unpublished master's thesis, Univ. of Washington, 1956.

Gough, H. G. A new dimension of status: I. Development of a personality scale. *Amer. sociol. Rev.*, 1948, 13, 401–409.

Gough, H. G., McClosky, H., and Meehl, P. E. A personality scale for dominance. *J. abnorm. soc. Psychol.*, 1951, 46, 360–366.

———. A personality scale for social responsibility. *J. abnorm. soc. Psychol.*, 1952, 47, 73–80.

Green, B. F. Attitude measurement. In G. Lindzey (Ed.), *Handbook of social psychology.* Vol. 1. *Theory and method.* Cambridge, Mass.: Addison-Wesley 1954. Pp. 335–469.

GUILFORD, J. P. *Psychometric methods.* (2nd Ed.) New York: McGraw-Hill, 1954.

———. *The Guilford-Martin Personnel Inventory. Manual of directions and norms.* Beverly Hills, Calif.: Sheridan Supply Co., undated.

HAMMOND, K. R. Measuring attitude by error-choice: An indirect method. *J. abnorm. soc. Psychol.,* 1948, 43, 38–48.

HANLEY, C. Social desirability and responses to items from three MMPI scales: *D, Sc,* and *K. J. appl. Psychol.,* 1956, 40, 324–328.

HASTINGS, P. K. A relationship between visual perception and level of personal insecurity. *J. abnorm. soc. Psychol.,* 1952, 47, 552–560.

HATHAWAY, S. R., and MCKINLEY, J. C. *Manual for the Minnesota Multiphasic Personality Inventory.* (Rev. Ed.) New York: Psychol. Corp., 1951.

HOLZMAN, P. S. The relation of assimilation tendencies in vision, auditory, and kinesthetic time-error to cognitive attitudes of leveling and sharpening. *J. Pers.,* 1954, 22, 375–394.

HOLZMAN, P. S., and KLEIN, G. S. Cognitive system-principles of leveling and sharpening: Individual differences in visual time-error. *J. Psychol.,* 1954, 37, 105–122.

KELLEHER, D. The construction of a measure of test-taking attitude on the Edwards Personal Preference Schedule. Unpublished master's thesis, Univ. of Washington, 1957.

KENNY, D. T. The influence of social desirability on discrepancy measures between real self and ideal self. *J. consult. Psychol.,* 1956, 20, 315–318.

KLETT, C. J. A study of the Edwards Personal Preference Schedule in relation to socio-economic status. Unpublished doctoral dissertation, Univ. of Washington, 1956.

———. The social desirability stereotype in a hospital population. *J. consult. Psychol.,* 1957, in press.

KLINEBERG, O. *Social psychology.* (Rev. Ed.) New York: Holt, 1954.

KOGAN, KATE, and KOGAN, W. S. Social desirability scale values of items in the Interpersonal Check List. Personal communication, 1957.

KOGAN, W. S., QUINN, R. D., AX, A. F., and RIPLEY, H. S. Some methodological problems in the quantification of clinical assessment by Q array. *J. consult. Psychol.,* 1956, 21, 57–62.

LAFORGE, R., and SUCZEK, R. F. The interpersonal dimension of personality: III. An Interpersonal Check List. *J. Pers.,* 1955, 24, 94–112.

LAMPHERE, A. V. The relationship between dependency factors and goal-setting behavior in duodenal ulcer patients. Unpublished doctor's dissertation, Univ. of Washington, 1953.

LAZARUS, R. S., ERIKSEN, C. W., and FONDA, C. P. Personality dynamics and auditory perceptual recognition. *J. Pers.*, 1951, 19, 471–482.

LEARY, T. *Manual for the Use of the Interpersonal System of Personality.* Berkeley, Calif.: Psychological Consultation Service, 1956.

LOVAAS, O. I. Comparison of social desirability ratings between Norwegian and American college students. Personal communication, 1956.

LUCAS, J. D. The interactive effects of anxiety, failure, and intraserial duplication. *Amer. J. Psychol.*, 1952, 65, 59–66.

MAINORD, W. A. An experimental approach to repression. Unpublished doctor's dissertation, Univ. of Washington, 1956.

MALLER, J. B. The effect of signing one's name. *Sch. and Soc.*, 1930, 31, 882–884.

MANDLER, G., and SARASON, S. B. A study of anxiety and learning. *J. abnorm. soc. Psychol.*, 1952, 47, 166–173.

MASLOW, A., *et al. Manual for the Security-Insecurity Inventory.* Stanford, Calif.: Stanford Univ. Press, 1952.

MCGINNIES, E. Emotionality and perceptual defense, *Psychol. Rev.*, 1949, 56, 244–251.

MEEHL, P. E. *Clinical vs. statistical prediction.* Minneapolis, Minn.: Univ. of Minn. Press, 1954.

MEEHL, P. E., and HATHAWAY, S. R. The K factor as a suppressor variable in the Minnesota Multiphasic Personality Inventory. *J. appl. Psychol.*, 1946, 30, 525–564.

MERRILL, R. M., and HEATHERS, LOUISE B. The relation of the MMPI to the Edwards Personal Preference Schedule on a college counseling center sample. *J. consult. Psychol.*, 1956, 20, 310–314.

MONTAGUE, E. K. The role of anxiety in serial rote learning. *J. exp. Psychol.*, 1953, 45, 91–96.

NAVRAN, L. A rationally derived MMPI scale to measure dependence. *J. consult. Psychol.*, 1954, 18, 192.

NAVRAN, L., and STAUFFACHER, J. C. Social desirability as a factor in Edwards Personality Preference Schedule performance. *J. consult. Psychol.*, 1954, 18, 442.

NEPRASH, J. A. The reliability of questions in the Thurstone Personality Schedule. *J. soc. Psychol.*, 1936, 7, 239–244.

OLSON, W. C. The waiver of signature in personal reports. *J. appl. Psychol.*, 1936, 20, 442–450.

ROSEN, E. Self-appraisal, personality desirability, and perceived social desirability of personality traits. *J. abnorm. soc. Psychol.*, 1956, 52, 151–158.

SARASON, S. B., MANDLER, G., and CRAIGHILL, P. G. The effect of differential instructions on anxiety and learning. *J. abnorm. soc. Psychol.*, 1952, 47, 561–565.

SCHLESINGER, H. G. Cognitive attitudes in relation to susceptibility to interference. *J. Pers.*, 1954, 22, 345–374.

SISSON, E. D. Forced choice–the new Army rating. *Personnel Psychol.*, 1948, 1, 365–381.

SPENCER, D. Frankness of subjects on personality measures. *J. educ. Psychol.*, 1938, 29, 26–35.

STEPHENSON, W. *The study of behavior.* Chicago: Univ. of Chicago Press, 1953.

STROTHER, C. R., and SCHAIE, K. W. Age differences in personality: A comparison of young and old age groups of superior ability. *Amer. Psychologist,* 1955, 10, 339. (Abstract.)

TAYLOR, D. M. Changes in the self concept without psychotherapy. *J. consult. Psychol.*, 1955, 19, 205–209.

TAYLOR, JANET A. A personality scale of manifest anxiety. *J. abnorm. soc. Psychol.*, 1953, 48, 285–290.

TAYLOR, JANET A., and SPENCE, K. W. The relationship of anxiety level to performance in serial learning. *J. exp. Psychol.*, 1952, 44, 61–64.

VERNON, P. E. *Personality tests and assessment.* New York: Holt, 1953.

WHEELER, W. M., LITTLE, K. B., and LEHNER, G. F. J. The internal structure of the MMPI. *J. consult. Psychol.*, 1951, 15, 134–141.

WIENER, D. R. Subtle and obvious keys for the Minnesota Multiphasic Personality Inventory. *J. consult. Psychol.*, 1948, 12, 164–170.

WINNE, J. F. A scale of neuroticism: An adaptation of the MMPI. *J. clin. Psychol.*, 1951, 7, 117–122.

WRIGHT, C. E. Relations between normative and ipsative measures of personality. Unpublished doctor's dissertation, Univ. of Washington, 1957.

ZIMMER, H. Self-acceptance and its relation to conflict. *J. consult. Psychol.*, 1954, 18, 447–449.

Index

Index

www.ingramcontent.com/pod-product-compliance
Lightning Source LLC
LaVergne TN
LVHW101441200926
848483LV00001B/9